NOW WE ARE FOUR

An Introduction to Early Childhood Education

NOW WE ARE FOUR

An Introduction to Early Childhood Education

Frederick N. Ebbeck
Riverina College of Advanced Education,
Wagga Wagga, New South Wales, Australia

Marjory A. Ebbeck
Riverina College of Advanced Education,
Wagga Wagga, New South Wales, Australia

CHARLES E. MERRILL PUBLISHING COMPANY
A Bell & Howell Company
Columbus, Ohio 43216

The author and publisher gratefully acknowledge Richard Farcus of the Division of Photographic Services of the University of Maryland for the use of his photographs which appear on pages 15, 65, 66, and 83.

372.21

Eb lN

117857

cyn. 1981

Published by
CHARLES E. MERRILL PUBLISHING COMPANY
A Bell & Howell Company
Columbus, Ohio 43216

Library of Congress Catalog Card Number: 73-89283

International Standard Book Number: 0-675-08856-9

1 2 3 4 5 6 7 8 9 10—78 77 76 75 74

Printed in the United States of America

PREFACE

The preschool years should be an exciting event in children's lives. They are at a stage in their development during which they rapidly expand their interests, abilities, and knowledge. It is a stage when they learn to become social beings. In many respects, being a pre-schooler is like being able to open a gate which leads out into an exciting, bubbling, busy world full of exciting things to do, to see, and to experience.

For some time, educators have appreciated the importance of quality education for young children. There have been many attempts in many parts of the world to provide this quality education, with varying degrees of success. All we can ask is for the teacher to read what we have written and to reflect upon it in the light of his or her own understanding of young children and their growth and development.

Throughout this book, we have attempted to show classroom practices which are consistent with our philosophy of educating young children. We believe:

That children are individuals.

That in order to learn, young children need to experience at a concrete level those things they are to learn.

That the environment fosters good experiences.

That children's perceiving is the unique and creating shaping of their world. They alone see with what they have seen; they alone experience with what they have experienced.

That fantasy, make-believe, and dramatization play a large and valuable part in the lives and development of children.

That the teacher has an active and personal role to play in assisting the developing children and their growing creativity.

We have divided the book into three parts. Part One sets out the philosophical and psychological theories underlying the methodology of teaching that comprises Parts Two and Three. Part Two elaborates what we see to be the two most important goals in early childhood education, namely, developing children's ability to communicate and to develop their understanding of their environment as they see it. In Part Three, we draw together the material from Part Two and show how it can be programmed for implementation in the classroom situation.

We are extremely grateful to our friend and colleague Dr. Harry Penny, of Adelaide, South Australia, for his help in the preparation of this book, for his reading of the manuscript and for his insightful comments regarding it. We also thank the various people who permitted us to photograph children at work and other aspects of preschool and kindergarten life.

Frederick Ebbeck
Marjory Ebbeck

CONTENTS

PART ONE: The Child   1

*Some Considerations
for Curriculum Design,* **3**
Children Are Individuals, **3**
Children and Their Motives, **5**
Children Grow through Play, **8**
Children and Their Learning, **15**
Readiness for New Tasks, **19**
*Implications for
Teaching: A Summary,* **23**
Bibliography, **27**

PART TWO: An Activity-Based
Curriculum   29

Introduction   30

SECTION A: The Development of Skills
of Communication   34

CHAPTER ONE: **The Development of Communication
                      through Language: A Product
                      of Growing and Experiencing**   **35**

                      *Each Child
                      Is Different,* **37**
                      *Providing Opportunities for
                      Children to Communicate
                      Verbally Effectively,* **38**
                      *Providing Opportunities to
                      Become Involved with
                      Written Communication,* **42**
                      Bibliography, **68**

CHAPTER TWO: **The Development of
                      Communication through
                      Music, Movement, and Dance**   **70**

                      Music, **74**
                      Movement, **79**
                      Drama, **82**
                      Summary, **85**
                      Bibliography, **85**

CHAPTER THREE: **The Development of
                      Communication through Art**   **86**

                      The Manipulative Stage, **86**
                      The Symbolic Stage, **87**
                      An Art Environment, **87**
                      *Setting the Scene for Art Work
                      with Young Children,* **89**
                      *What Art Experiences Should
                      We Offer to Young Children?,* **94**
                      Group Experiences in Art, **101**
                      Summary, **101**
                      Bibliography, **102**

SECTION B: The Development of an Awareness
             and Understanding of
             the Environment   **104**

CHAPTER FOUR: Introduction   **105**

CHAPTER FIVE: The Development of an Understanding
                 of Mathematics in the Child's Environment

                 108

                 Planning the Curriculum, **108**
                 Provision of Materials, **113**
                 Summary, **114**
                 Bibliography, **115**

CHAPTER SIX: The Development of an Understanding of
                 Science in the Child's Environment   **116**

                 Recording Children's Science, **128**
                 *Materials Which Will Help the Young
                 Child Understand His Environment,* **128**
                 Bibliography, **130**

CHAPTER SEVEN: The Development of an Understanding
                 of the Child's Social Environment   **132**

                 Teachers and Their Task, **136**
                 Summary, **138**
                 Bibliography, **138**

PART THREE: The Child and
              His Curriculum   **141**

                 The Role of the Teacher, **144**

Integrated Day, **144**
Daily and Long-Term Planning, **148**
Classroom Organization, **154**
Record Keeping of Pupil Progress, **160**
Working with Parents, **164**

APPENDIX A: **Bibliography of Children's Books** 172

APPENDIX B: **Recipes Suitable for Use in Classrooms** 177

Homemade Bread, **179**
Homemade Condensed Milk, **179**
Buttermilk Cheese, **180**
Fruit Salad Jam, **180**
Plain Cake, **180**
Meringues, **181**
Cupcakes, **181**
Doughnuts, **181**
Peanut Cookies, **182**
No-Bake Hedge-Hog Slices, **182**
Bumble Bees, **182**
Simple Cookie Mixture, **183**
Shortbread, **183**
Old Fashioned Sugar Cookies, **183**
Candy, **184**
Jello Cubes, **186**
Marshmallows, **186**

INDEX   **189**

PART ONE

The
Child

SOME CONSIDERATIONS
FOR CURRICULUM DESIGN

No matter what curriculum design is used by teachers in their day-by-day teaching, it is essential that there be some basic philosophical and psychological theory underlying the particular design. It is the purpose of this section to outline the theories which underly the practices elaborated on in Parts Two and Three.

We have divided Part One into subsections which deal with important determiners in guiding our understanding of the behavior of young children. It is only through such an understanding that we can meaningfully provide, in a school setting, for their needs. No one subsection is dealt with in great detail, for to do so would demand at least a full length chapter for each. Instead, a bibliography is provided at the end of this part, and the reader is invited to pursue his interests further by selecting readings from the bibliography.

CHILDREN ARE
INDIVIDUALS

To be a successful teacher of young children, one must be knowledgeable about them. Such knowledge should be about each child and his needs; it is a knowledge of how he grows and develops, of his interests and his desires, of his abilities and his progress, and of the ways by which he learns.

What, then, do we know about children? To begin, we know that no two children are exactly alike—and that this is true even of "identical" twins. We know that children of the same age vary greatly in physique—in weight, height, stamina—and that these variations continue and indeed increase as children grow older. We know that in general girls develop physically earlier than boys and that girls are more able to cope with physical illnesses than boys. We know, too, that physical growth is sequential in that it progresses for every individual in an orderly sequence which, in a broad sense, is common to all children.

We know that children differ markedly in personality and character. For many years, it has been claimed by some that genetic inheritance is quite the most important determiner of the child's level of intelligence and of his personality and character. It is now more widely believed that environmental influences play a substantial part in the development—or frustration of development—of the potentialities of each child; that personality and character are profoundly shaped by the culture, and, indeed, by the subculture within which the child lives and grows. The culture defines the limits of acceptable and nonacceptable behavior.

The family, of course, is—at least for a while—a powerful influence in molding the personality and character of its members. But in this modern age, when the composition of families as well as of the culture itself is changing, it is becoming increasingly difficult for the child as he grows older to be able to recognize what are deemed "acceptable" models of stable personality and character by his society. In many cases, the child is turning away from his family in his search for this acceptable model and is becoming more and more influenced by his peer groups.

In summary, we can say first that personality differences among children in any culture or subculture are dependent upon the interaction of inherited differences of temperament and inherited factors in intelligence with differences in family style, upbringing, and environment. Second, much of the child's behavior is the result of his being influenced from within his peer group.

We know that children differ in *abilities,* not only with regard to those abilities which demand cognitive processes but also in those abilities which require manipulative dexterity and a degree of motor coordination. For example, some children we teach are considered awkward in movement, while others are graceful. Some children can sing well; others sing not at all well.

Children differ markedly in their *interests,* in the way they become *motivated* and sustain this motivation, and also in the way in which they grasp new *learning.* These matters are dealt with more fully later in this part.

What we are saying is that children are individuals and because they are individuals, each child is unique. Teachers have known this simple yet extremely important fact for a long time; but not many have sufficiently heeded it, not so much in what they say but in what they do. The very act of slavishly following a class textbook page after page without thought of the needs and interests and abilities of each child in the class or of having an entire class work at the same assignment at the same time are perfect and, unfortunately, commonplace examples of such ignoring of individuals and their differences. If we are aware of and heed the fact that individual differences among children appear very early in life, then as teachers of young children, we can better plan a curriculum and adjust our teaching procedures to the individual. In such a way, we help each child. It is just as vital that this be done in preschools as in elementary schools. The thesis of this book is that teachers need to be knowledgeable about children if they are to be able to *prescribe* and *provide* for the needs of each child.

One further point of view concerning the individualizing of our teaching stems from the fact that *all learning is individual*. It has to be, for it is always the individual and never "the class" who does the learning—who memorizes, or not; understands, or not; appreciates, or not. The essence of our discussion of individualization in our classrooms is not the separation of child from child on what is sometimes described as a one-to-one basis—that is, one child to one teacher. This is impossible to do in a normal classroom. Rather, it is the quality of the attention and perseverance *evidenced by each child* in the solving of a problem or the working to perfect a skill. The teacher must exercise a strong pervasive influence over her whole class if she is to be able to individualize her teaching. If her influence is not pervasive then little effective learning will be done by the twenty-nine youngsters who are going about their learning tasks while the teacher is attending to the individual needs of the thirtieth child.

CHILDREN AND
THEIR MOTIVES

A *motive* is an inner moving or impelling power. It is an urge to do something. One such urge is to learn. We have all seen young babies, before they are able to walk, pull themselves up on furniture in their homes, fall down, and pull themselves up again and again. Older children, when learning to ride a bicycle, strive and strive for mastery over the difficult feat of balancing on two wheels. They will endure the usually frequent falls for the sake of learning to ride. Adults will work diligently at something they want to master—golf or chess, for example. Most adults, too, will endure setbacks and other problems associated with learning a task that interests them.

Naturally, the direction an urge takes differs between old and young and between people of similar ages, but the urge to learn is real nevertheless.

We all know of experiments in which plants, given varying amounts of daylight at various angles, will lean and grow in the direction of the daylight. They do so because they need daylight to live and have a built-in mechanism which directs growth toward fulfilling a basic need. Similarly, there are basic needs which man must fulfill if he is to exist. He needs food, water, love. There is the urge to propagate his kind, and so on. Such needs may be called *primary motives.*

Man also has an urge to do things and to become somebody. Such urges call forth energies which direct him toward the achievement of his goals beyond those described above as being primary. These motives are called *secondary* for they have been modified as a result of individual experiences within the context of a given culture. Teachers are concerned with these secondary motives because working with and through them, they are more likely to interest children in learning. When an interest in learning exists, it can be tapped and directed.

It is fair enough to say that not all children want to learn what is expected of them to learn. Although many children, like adults, procrastinate and will so delay their learning, it is fair enough to say, too, that the better teachers are more able to arouse the interest of individual children and, even if they are initially reticent, lead them into involvement in learning situations.

One way by which teachers involve their children in their work is through the use of competition. We do not think that fostering the competitive urge in children, as is generally done in elementary and secondary schools, has a place in the education of four- and five-year-old children. We mean that kind of competition, especially in cognitive learning experiences, which sets child against child in what is frequently an uneven match. However, if competition is used in a personal way—that is, if the young child is competing against himself, striving to better his own ability—then results are good. The whole question of competition as a stimulus to learning with young children is a delicate one, and we feel we must repeat our statement that it is better ignored in preschools and kindergartens.

In school situations, teachers spend a great deal of their time introducing new materials to their children in a variety of ways. Naturally, not all children will be equally interested in new material merely because it is new. As we have said, learner interest is a vital factor in effective learning, and, therefore, the teacher must somehow stimulate an interest in the learning task at hand. There is no easy way to do this. Teachers can only hope that in organizing learning situations, the methods they use to create a learning environment and *their own obvious interest* in what is being learned will quicken the child's imagination and will encourage the child to become curious. This, in turn, will lead to a genuine interest in the new material. In this way, an interest in learning, especially "school" learning, is likely to be developed in the child. A teacher genuinely interested in the child and in his learning engenders interest in the child she teaches.

What does this discussion of motivation mean for the teacher? *First,* teachers need to get to know their children as quickly as possible—their interests, what they are adequate at doing (that is, what they can do well and *know* that they can do well) and what they are inadequate at (that is, what they cannot do well but would like to do well). It is only when teachers know their children that they can prescribe for their needs. It is not what a child finds himself unable to do that hurts him. Rather, it is when inability is associated with the idea that he is a failure, with the accompanying self-uncertainty and even humiliation, that inability passes into the destructive view of the self as inadequate. Such feelings of inadequacy have to be worked on first if we want to guide the behavior of the child into a positive direction.

Second, we need to become aware of what interests children and then work through these interests to greater learning. This "working through" interests is never ending, for one interest leads to another, to another, and so on. The teacher who has a particular goal in mind—that of deepening a child's knowledge, understanding, and skills—will need to direct interests along certain paths. The classroom catering to the interests of a number of developing children must provide a richly stimulating environment, but it is rich only if it is varied and constantly varying. It is stimulating only to the extent that whatever is available makes some appeal to the children (though the younger the children the less likely it will be for the "same" object or activity to catch and hold the interest of all the children at the same time). In other words, a classroom which attempts to stimulate all the children's interests is an ever-changing one where materials are assembled and reassembled as the demand for them dictates and are put away when their purpose is finished.

CHILDREN GROW
THROUGH PLAY

Susan Isaacs has stated that whoever has the power to understand children's play holds the key to understanding their development. It is unfortunate that in the past educators have tended to regard play as being valuable chiefly as therapy or as a form of social development or, worse, as the opposite of serious and useful activity. The former two viewpoints of the value of play are important, certainly, but so is play valuable in cognitive development. It is an aspect of education too long neglected except perhaps in specialized "remedial" programs. As teachers, we should give weight to each of three aspects of play—therapeutic, social, and cognitive—if we are to understand the great value of play in the total learning of the whole child.

Even though we are going to consider each of these three aspects of play separately, it is probably true, and it should be mentioned here, that the child does not consider them separately. Indeed, Lois Murphy in her studies of and experiments with seven-year-old children found that the intellectual and social processes in games were really aspects of a single growth process.[1] This point of view is in keeping with the teaching of both Piaget and Erikson, two great educators who have helped us to understand the development of young children. They have, each from his own viewpoint, divided human growth into stages and have described play as being developmental, expressing the function and needs of the growing child.

Play is the young child's first and fundamental means for development. A child's earliest play, in which he explores and experiences his immediate environment is manipulative in nature. He manipulates what is encompassed in his environment. In this way, the child grows to know his environment because of his experiences in and of it. Later, his play progresses through stages of make-believe symbolic play to more complicated symbolic play which incorporates rules and structure until, in adolescence, we see his play taking on a more *obvious* intellectual form.

Let us look now more closely at the three aspects of play.

Play as a Therapeutic Agent

Clinical psychologists use play therapy as a means by which children work out inner problems; it is a structured way of dealing with

---

[1] Barbara Biber, Lois Barclay Murphy, et al., *Child Life in School* (New York: E. P. Dutton & Co., 1942).

problems. A sandbox or a doll's house may be used in a play situation. Whatever the objects used, however, their makeup is secondary to the diagnostic and then the therapeutic intention. Play materials can be used so that the child has something to do with his hands and can direct his attention to what he is doing, thereby avoiding direct confrontation with the therapist. Yet, again, a play therapist may have other purposes in mind when using objects in therapy play. Such purposes can be diagnostic or cathartic in nature.

In play therapy, the therapist realizes that children do not use language as adults would use it nor do they understand things as adults do. The success of the therapy cannot be judged by accepting a too literal meaning of the language the child uses during his play. Rather, it is the observed change occurring in the child's behavior during his out-of-therapy activities which is important in diagnosing the success or failure of the therapy.

Another aspect of play therapy which is important for teachers to consider is the degree of consistency or stability in the child's immediate surroundings, in this case his therapy room. The child is able at the beginning of each visit to continue his play where he previously left off at the end of his last session. He is not expected at each visit to start all over again or to begin a new activity.

Why should teachers understand play therapy? Though teachers are not trained therapists, they are able to provide therapeutic play experiences for young children in their classrooms. The following points provide a partial answer to the question and indicate a therapeutic role for the teacher.

1. Provision must be made in classrooms for play. Such provision includes not only materials but also extended periods of time during each day for children to *become absorbed in personal play.* Too often, teachers relegate play periods as "fill-ins" to keep children occupied between lessons or to keep them out of the way while other children finish their "seat" work. Such "play periods" are, in most cases, too short in duration for any worthwhile activity to be generated.

2. The teacher should be alert to use therapeutic play as a means of avoiding behavior problems. Such play activities could be planned before or after school or during lunch breaks if time cannot be found during the work day.

3. Children are sometimes happy to talk while they play and may appreciate having their teacher as a friendly listener. But

teachers (and parents) should certainly not try to prod children into explaining the meanings of their play. This kind of adult interference in child's play is frequently more harmful than good, for it focuses his attention on *what he is doing* to the detriment of the imaginative elements in his play.

4. There should be continuity in the play experiences of young children. It is disturbing to the child to experience too frequent changes in room layout and reorganization of material. Yet, on the other hand, it is just as detrimental to healthy play to have no change, no new material introduced, no old material removed from the play area. In this regard, there must be a balance achieved.

5. Too frequent changes of rooms for class activities and teachers for special subjects can be disturbing for the young child. Preschools and the primary grades of our public schools are not the best places to try out complicated team-teaching or differentiated staffing schemes which require both children and teachers to move too frequently during each day.

Play in the Socialization of the Child

Probably the most important socializing value of play is that children, as members of a group, begin to learn to understand each other by playing together. Indeed, it is as a member of a group that the individual forms certain attitudes, ideals and behaviors toward others. Margaret Lowenfeld has referred to this assuming of attitudes and ideals as an *adaptive process* which ". . . must continue throughout life and which profoundly affects man's ability to survive in his physical universe and ever-changing social environments." [2]

Attitudes, ideals, opinions, and language as part of man's social behavior are shaped by one's culture and, of course, the subculture to which one belongs. One has only to observe children at play in a ghetto area of a large inner city and to compare their play with that of their more affluent counterparts in the suburbs of the same city to appreciate fully the cultural differences in play and the tremendous power which cultures have over the development of the young. Play is a vital means by which young children become acculturated.

---

[2] Margaret Lowenfeld, *Play in Childhood* (New York: John Wiley & Sons, Inc., 1967), p. 7.

In the social development of young children, the parent and the teacher are concerned that each child participate as a member of a group. Observers of children at play know that children usually go through successive stages in their social play, from solitary play to parallel play to cooperative or group play. It is generally held that cooperative play begins around the child's third year, though preschool and kindergarten teachers know that there are many variations from this age.

Teachers foster social play because they appreciate its importance in the development of a child's personality. Lowenfeld has discussed the abilities and characteristics necessary if a child is to enter into and to enjoy social play. In summary, these characteristics are a spontaneous desire for association with other human beings; fluidity of emotion (i.e., swiftly changing emotional attitudes appropriate to children at play); a capacity to accept form in play; a capacity to follow a rule; a capacity to subordinate one's own wishes to the wishes of the group; a capacity to get emotional release out of identification with a group; and a capacity for love of one's fellows.[3]

This list of personal characteristics is rather formidable, but it must be remembered that a child's personality is the result of his interaction with his environment which in school includes, very importantly, others of about his age. It is by joining well in social play that he develops and confirms the very desirable personal characteristics described by Lowenfeld. It needs to be kept in mind though that each child will develop at his own pace and in his own ways. Nowhere more than in play are children individuals.

Hand in hand with a child's social development through play is his emotional development. We know that a young child is swept by his emotions. More frequently than not, he cannot easily control them. It has long been recognized that through play situations, children are able to work out many of their emotional problems. It is one of the major concerns of the teacher to help each child in her care to learn how to deal with his feelings, for as a child grows older, his social and emotional life not only becomes more complex, it needs to be more under his control and more organically structured. It is therefore imperative that a sound foundation for healthy social living be laid in the early years of preschool and formal schooling. The teacher has a definite role to play, for as with all learning, a child's social and emotional development is greatly dependent upon the guidance of the adult figures with whom he regularly comes into contact.

---

[3] Lowenfeld, pp. 240-46.

The importance for curriculum making and teaching practices of an awareness of the value of play in the social development of young children can be summarized as follows:

1. A realization that much of the social behavior of children is the result of their learning as a member of a group at play is essential.

2. Attitudes, beliefs, customs, goals, ideals, language, etc. are learned through play and have cultural values. It is through social play that significant cultural mores are communicated to children.

3. Through social play children are able to understand other people and their own position and role as a member of a social group. They are able to explore their differing roles; to come to grips with their emotions; and to rationalize, and hopefully to modify, their behavior in light of their cultural expectations.

Play as an Agent in Cognitive Development

A group of educational psychologists, namely the cognitive developmentalists, believe that play is the child's natural way of coming to terms with what in the adult world is called reality. For the young child play is reality and through play he discovers himself and his environment and learns to manipulate and to evaluate it. On the surface the child's play may appear to be merely pleasurable but underneath this surface there may be more complicated, intellectual thinking.

When considering the value of play in cognitive development, there needs to be a distinction made between *spontaneous play,* which is inner-directed with the child manipulating his environment to meet his *own* needs and for his own sake in a manner determined by his own logic, and *directed* or *structured play,* which is play instigated and directed by adults with goals predetermined by adults.

Spontaneous play takes various forms. There is the imaginative play of the *make-believe* where the child is identifying himself with someone in a particular situation. Make-believe play is often extremely vivid and rich. A child's choice of subject and materials for play and the way he uses them is usually an indicator of his intellectual maturity. Other factors, such as the child's sex, age, and interests, also govern the direction of his make-believe play. A five-year-old boy, for example, will choose differently from a five-year-old girl. The two-, three- or four-year-old child will have differing interests according to his stage of development.

Play stimulates intellectual growth in many ways. It causes a child to observe and to compare. In play the child makes use of his real life experiences so that his make-believe play becomes true to life. This is a form of reflecting, which in turn, develops understanding. Imaginative play also permits the child to experiment with solutions to problems. Susan Isaacs calls this kind of playing "as if-ness", where the child is learning to work out the consequences of hypothetical action without it being real.[4] Piaget regards this kind of play as basic to the development of logical thinking.

A second form of spontaneous play is that of the *fantasy*, or the *daydream*. Such play usually begins when the child is about six years old. Often private fantasies which are used for problem solving are highly romantic where the hero or the heroine of the "inner story" go through much complicated planning and reasoning in order to achieve his or her purpose.

A third form of imaginative play is that of the *imaginary companion*, important in the life of some six- and seven-year-old children—and even older. This imaginary person may be an intimate part of the life of the child, sharing his everyday experiences and ever ready to help in difficult situations. Such a "person" affords the child opportunities to talk out, as it were, problems and conflicts and tensions which might otherwise be disabling.

One should also consider the cognitive value of *directed play*. As stated earlier, directed play is instigated and directed by others, usually adults—parents and teachers. The aim, or intended goal of directed play is predetermined by the adult. The amount of direction varies from mere suggestion by the adult of what is to be done and the materials to be used to prescription of the activity, its rules and required outcomes. Whether or not this kind of closely directed activity can, as some educators believe, be called play, will depend not upon what the adult calls it but upon the spirit with which the child enters upon and continues the activity.

The older children become the more they need, and gain from, structured play. In other words the structuring of play is not in itself bad. It is the premature or unnecessary or bossy prescribing that is bad.

It should be mentioned that structured play often brings with it the element of competition. The more structured the play of two

---

[4] Susan Isaacs, *Childhood and After* (New York: International Universities Press, 1949), p. 58.

or more children the greater is the likelihood of the element of competition. In free or non-directed play, however, we believe that children, especially and very rightly young children, attach little significance to who wins or who loses. Nor do they require the stimulus of prizes to keep them playing. However, this is not the case with many of children's efforts to do well in our adult-directed schooling which is evoked and sustained far too much by an unhealthy use of the competitiveness usually to be found among children in "modern" cultures.

Much of what is called play in schools is so organized that experiences are structured for desired outcomes. This is particularly noticeable in mathematics teaching where, for example, the development of certain concepts is facilitated through play. Here the "exploration" of the properties of objects is done in the manner of play. Much of Piaget's thinking on how children learn has become basic theory for most of the modern mathematics curricula and many teachers have been trying to organize or structure situations in line with this thinking. A prime example is the development of spatial relations where it is necessary for teachers to structure situations by using certain equipment so that children, through play, will come to an understanding of their own position in space.

Structured play may have great value in the development of cognitive learning, especially in "school" education. Its value depends not only upon the amount of structuring done but also, and greatly, upon the manner and intensity of the child's involvement in the learning process. Structured play which inhibits the child's creativeness and which causes him to be more imitative is of negative educational value. Piaget, according to Almy,[5] suggests that over structured play may even inhibit the development of logical thinking, especially for young children. Obviously we must allow the child more time in our classrooms for spontaneous play and be ready to utilize the outcomes of this play. These periods of freedom should be continued throughout the school life of the child.

The importance of play in the cognitive development of young children can be summarized for teachers as follows:

A. Spontaneous play:

1. Gives the child the opportunity *in his own way* and *in his own time* to come to grips with problems which have not yet become clear to him.

---

[5] Millie Almy, "Spontaneous Play: An Avenue for Intellectual Development," *The Bulletin of the Institute of Child Study* 28 (November 1966).

2. Is a perfect form for the repetitive use of acquired knowledge and skills.
3. Allows, in a nonthreatening way, for the creation of new problems to be solved and skills to be developed which lead on from those which already have been mastered.
4. Provides situations where the child can observe, analyze and compare.
5. Allows, through make-believe, for a stretching of the child's mind through unpressured use of the imagination.

B. Directed play:
1. Introduced wisely, is indispensable if we are to guide children through those more systematic experiences that lead to more conceptual forms of learning, although it should be kept in mind that the younger the child the more useful for his development is undirected play.

CHILDREN AND THEIR LEARNING

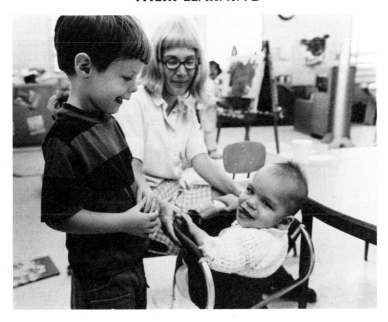

A Nursery School for Very Young Children

All good thinkers about the educating of young children believe strongly in the importance of activity and discovery in children's learning. We have only to read the writings of Susan Isaacs, the Macmillan sisters, Rachael and Margaret, Margaret Lowenfeld, and before them Pestalozzi (1746-1827), Froebel (1782-1852) and Dewey (1859-1952), to appreciate that this belief in active participation in learning is far from a new creed among educators whether of younger or older children or of adults. Yet this belief and certainly its practice are not as widespread as should be. Rather, many teachers guide their children into "formalized" learning as quickly as possible in the mistaken belief that young children learn best this way. The belief permeating this book is that children need to be *active* participants in their learning rather than passive receptacles waiting to be filled with knowledge and learning.

From studies of how people learn we see that learning is a continuous process and that it has to be an active process. It is active because there is a continuous struggle by the learner to master his environment. We know from studies of psychology that a child is born into the world with a potential for becoming human, that is, a potential for learning; but it is his interaction with his environment—all that he comes into contact with once he is born—that modifies this innate potential. This is why a teacher is so important in a child's life. She, the teacher, is important because of what she can *do* to improve the child's learning environment by providing him with challenging opportunities to progress, to learn. Later in this book, we will consider how the teacher can structure the learning environment of the school so that from the opportunities she provides the child, a stable pattern of growth through learning will prevail.

To the question: how do children learn? we could say they learn:

   . . . as the result of being curious. Children are actively curious, forever exploring with fingers and tongues and eyes, asking questions and probing into the "why's" and "what-for's" of living. This process could be called *inquiry.*

   . . . by imitating other people. The ways children develop their speaking accent and adopt the idioms of their mother language is a good example of imitation.

   . . . by experimenting. One example of learning in this way is the boy who, when working with clay, hit the lump of clay against the edge of the table and noticed the interesting design he got. He then went on to see what kinds of impressions or designs in the clay other objects would leave.

. . . through nonverbal communication. We all know of the power of the "silent-language", the "body language"— gesture, signs, facial expressions—and how quickly the child will receive and develop a personal meaning from them.

. . . by associating experiences. It does not take long for a child to associate certain stimuli with something he already has learned. For example, a child in nursery school will come to connect the properties of objects with their ability to float on water.

But over all of these modes of learning are two factors which singly are more important yet each one pervades all the others. They are:

. . . children learn when they are interested in their activities, and

. . . children learn through experiencing things.

We have spoken at length about motivation earlier in this Part. Interests and motives go hand in hand; in other words they complement each other. Yet in this highly mechanized and scientific society of ours where there is so much to learn, we cannot hope that all children will become equally interested in the same aspect of learning at the same time and to the same degree. This fact has importance for curriculum planning. As Dearden [6] argued, one should consider the interests of children when planning programs of work but the teacher should also keep in mind that children's interests at any given time cannot be the sole criterion for program construction. The teacher should not only be mindful of the *direction* of children's interests—direction here being the point to which the interests are leading—but she must also keep clearly in mind the aims and purposes of the school in relation to society at large if schooling is to be educative and not, as Dewey said, miseducative. The role of the teacher in this respect is simple to state yet not so simple to achieve. It is to devise means by which children will, of their own accord as it were, become interested in the task at hand. The teacher needs to become a saleswoman using every wile in her power to convince her buyers that her product is needed. But, and most important, her product needs to be good.

The second all embracing factor in children's learning, that children learn by experiencing, needs some elaboration here. This, indeed,

---

[6] R. F. Dearden, *The Philosophy of Primary Education* (London: Routledge and Kegan Paul, 1968), pp. 22-23.

is what this book is about. Learning by experiencing is the way in which concepts are developed. It is not true to say, as many teachers do, that their task is to teach children concepts of this or that. If by "teaching" is meant that the child learns what the teacher says, then concepts cannot be learned. A concept is an abstract idea and as such has to be grasped. Indeed, the abstracting itself (the process indispensable to the generating of a concept) must be actively achieved by the child. If the concept is to be a clear and powerful one then it can only be the learner who does the abstracting and grasping. The teacher can, and it is her task to, generate situations or to structure the environment which will lead the learner to the point where an idea or concept is developed within his mind. And the good teacher does this in many ways, each of which leads the learner through an experience to a better understanding of the concept, and as a result to becoming increasingly confident in his own abilities.

It is important for sound learning that the teacher so arranges the learning environment that the learner is led to perceive order in his experiences. We can, for example, appreciate the orderly progression from the insect world to the study of spiders (or vice versa) and see the possibilities for incidental mathematical learning which could arise through developing the study along experiential and experimental as opposed to merely verbal lines. Art, music, stories (the children's as well as published ones) and other means of communication can be part of the total experience generated from the original topic—insects and spiders. The opposite of this approach is the preordained, detailed prescription, day by day, of new topics. This is the traditional form of curriculum design where one day (or week) spiders are studied, the next day (or week) the topic could be outer space. There is no inherent reason, however, why there should not be leaps of this kind—provided that the leaping arises from what concerns the children.

Whatever scheme we follow for the planning of learning experiences for young children we must not bewilder them by chopping and changing topics, by too fast or too slow a speed of development, or by going so far beyond their past experiences that the new material is beyond their comprehension. If it is, then of course it is not "material" for the child. We need to remember that for new experiences to be meaningful they need to be in some way related to the child's previous experiences.

One last point for consideration at this stage is that teachers, when structuring the learning environment, must provide rich and varied materials and situations so that much experiencing towards the generating of the concept is gained in and through a variety of situations.

READINESS FOR NEW TASKS

A young baby does a vast amount of practicing when preparing for the "walking stage". A ceaseless striving of pulling up, standing, walking around furniture goes on and on. The falls and knocks sustained by the baby during this practice do not deter or diminish the strong desire to succeed. The repetition is constant yet boredom never exists. One does observe over the weeks, however, a refinement of movement, an increased confidence and, finally, an *emergence of readiness* for the next step.

The young child of four years who has had the opportunity to paint at an easel will do so confidently and boldly. The products of these early attempts probably will have little visual meaning to the observer and indeed may represent nothing more than large patches of color. However, the child will be absorbed, intent and enjoying the fluid media and the physical manipulation of the brush and paint. If the child is given numerous opportunities to experiment and manipulate and is free from adult interference of a prescriptively directing kind, it is fascinating to notice the development of readiness. What is represented in the child's art takes on the appearance of, and as well becomes, a meaningful expression of what the child is attempting to communicate.

These are two examples of one aspect of readiness—a factor in learning. We refer to this aspect as the *emergence of readiness,* though it should be kept clearly in mind that the process of becoming ready is usually lengthy. From one point of view it is the culmination of all previous experiences in a particular area of learning, but looking forward, it signals the readiness of the child to attempt to master something new—a new skill or some new knowledge.

Readiness has been defined as:

> The capability for meeting successfully certain expectancies for achieving particular levels of performance.[7]

---

[7] Richard M. Brandt, "The Readiness Issue Today," *The Record* 71 (February 1970): 440.

If we accept this definition, then readiness means that the child is at the stage where he can learn effectively without undue frustration and yet be challenged and stimulated in the process of striving for success. Readiness is still a term which is misunderstood and misinterpreted by teachers. For one teacher it may be the consideration of certain factors on a readiness checklist which assess whether a child is ready to benefit or not from a particular learning experience. For another teacher, who believes that you can make the child fit the program, readiness is a relatively unimportant consideration. To yet another teacher, readiness may mean looking at the total development of the child and making an appraisal of what his reaction to a particular learning experience is likely to be. If we go back to our definition of readiness we see it is that necessary stage in a child's development which shows that he is able to cope successfully with new learning. Like any other stage, it requires careful consideration on the part of the teacher of several factors which together constitute that "stage."

Many teachers believe that it is difficult to recognize signs of readiness in the child *at the crucial time*. We know that for each individual child there is an optimum time, a "best time", and that teachers have to use their own judgment based on observation and careful appraisal when determining whether or not a child is ready to begin a learning task. A checklist, used wisely, can be very helpful.

Because of societal and school needs and pressures, reading readiness always has been, and still is, the prime concern of teachers of young children. If a child exhibits maturity in all relevant areas of development and has a strong desire to learn to read, then obviously the time to start reading is "now". To delay reading and continue to concentrate the child's efforts on some specific "readiness skill" may lead to his frustration and at a later stage, indifference. Most teachers have encountered the eager five-year-old whose sole desire in the first few weeks of formal school is to "learn to read". If he is both eager and ready to begin to learn to read, it is surely a mistake to require the child to spend weeks and weeks on ditto sheets of readiness exercises, just because the teacher has them at hand. To do so diminishes, perhaps seriously, the *desire* to read, a fundamental factor of readiness.

The other extreme exists too, where very young and immature children have been taught to read, sometimes with apparently spectacular results. However, research [8] shows that there is little to be

---

[8] The reader is directed to the article by Nila Banton Smith, "Early Reading: Viewpoints," in *Early Childhood: Crucial Years for Learning* (Washington, D.C.: Association for Childhood Education International, 1966), pp. 60-64, for a discussion on related research.

gained by starting children on some learning task before they are ready for it. The spectacular results cited in many reading experiments are often limited to selected children in controlled situations and there is little evidence that these children are able to apply the skills learned in reading to other learning situations. Undue pressure placed on young children to learn when they are not ready for it often results in the development of poor attitudes towards learning.

Ann Fryer, though she is talking specifically about reading readiness, says something that is true of readiness in general:

> It is easy to be concerned when a child takes a long time to achieve reading readiness, especially when anxious parents appear to place responsibility for his non-reading on you, the teacher. But, if you can be confident that you are giving this child every opportunity and that in your professional judgment it would be wrong to try and push things because of later consequences, then you can better reassure parents who are not trained teachers that you too have the best interests of their child at heart; and you can give them a picture of his present stage of development and how you are catering for it.[9]

The school environment must allow each child the opportunity to grow and develop. It must be broad enough in scope to meet the individual child's needs and be stimulating enough to arouse in each child the desire to learn. If the child at six or seven is still not ready for formal reading then this should not be viewed as a tragedy, nor should the child be made to feel a failure and sent out as such to a reading specialist. Schools would be healthier, too, if some teachers and parents realized that slowness in learning to read is not by any means a certain and sad indication of below average intelligence. Experiences must be planned which will aid the development of reading and yet be meaningful and worthwhile to the child. The teacher's role in this is critical.

It is unfortunate that some teachers are over-concerned with getting young children into the formal stages of learning to read. As a result reading readiness has become another subject which teachers teach, often irrespective of whether or not a child can profit from it or, indeed, needs a readiness program at all. This is unintelligent of the teacher and grievous for the child. There is nothing like the same concern with readiness in areas other than reading. This does not mean that readiness in any of these areas of learning is any less important. The decision as to readiness in math, writing

---

[9] Ann Fryer, "Teaching Reading in the Infant School," in *Teaching in the British Primary School*, ed. V. R. Rogers (New York: The Macmillan Co., 1971), pp. 110-11.

and other areas of communication depends on the teacher's ability to recognize by observation what each child is doing, saying and wanting to do. In math, for example, Piaget, who has greatly influenced our knowledge of young children and their methods of acquiring knowledge and skills, has urged upon us the need to observe the signs in children's behavior which indicate sufficient mastery of a given concept or skill before proceeding to the next task in a sequence of learning. He also clearly set out for us, as results of his experiments with children's thinking, the steps in the process of children's thinking and what children can be expected to attain at each stage in their development.

In general, when trying to assess the readiness of the child for any learning task there are certain factors which need to be considered. These are:

The stage of maturity reached by the child. This refers to the physical, mental and social growth and development of the child. An example can again be seen in readiness for reading. To begin reading the child must be capable of expressing simple ideas; his vision must be sufficiently developed so that he can see differences between what are to us letters and printed words; he must be able to listen discriminately in order to hear fine differences in sounds in words; he must be able to concentrate for short periods without undue strain and fatigue; and he must be able to recall experiences in some form of sequential episodes.

Experiential background of the child. Here we need to consider the child's home and neighborhood environment and the type of experiences they provide. The child who has had a wide background of meaningful experiences at home is more likely to achieve success in learning tasks, and to succeed earlier, than other children whose experience has been in more "deprived" (i.e., culturally and socially restricted) home environments.

Ideally, the home and school environment should fully and richly complement one another. This is, unfortunately, rarely the case. Therefore it is essential that the teacher consider the experiential background of each child in her class if she is to develop experiences in the curriculum which will cater to his needs. The home environment of the child is beyond the control of the teacher but such is not true of the school environment. The school environment must be enriching so that it not only complements the home but allows the child to experience things which may in some important fields be far beyond what he is able to get at home.

Motivation. Motivation is another influential factor in readiness. Although a child can be physically and mentally mature and have opportunities to learn a task, he will not learn unless he is motivated to do so. As mentioned earlier in this Part, we have all seen the determination and persistence a child exhibits when he is mastering the difficult task of learning to ride a bicycle. Most children are highly motivated, and very very few fail to learn to ride. The same cannot be said of learning to read.

In summary, the ultimate responsibility for deciding when the child is ready for a school learning task rests with the individual teacher, and such a decision can wisely be made only after considering the total development of the whole child. She might want to check the development of the child against a series of questions about the child, which together could take the form of a checklist such as the one below, although the value of any checklist will depend upon the extent to which the teacher gets to know each child intimately through close observation of his growing and developing behavior.

1. Is the child able to converse fluently?
2. Can he communicate simple personal needs?
3. Can he listen to and carry out simple directions?
4. Can he perform skills that involve muscular coordination?
5. Can he work and play with other children without intense frustration?
6. Does he show an interest in the environment around him?
7. Is he willing to become involved in group activities, e.g., art, music and story time?
8. Can he observe with reasonable accuracy?
9. Can he concentrate on a task for a short time without undue fatigue?
10. Does he exhibit independence in selecting for himself a task he wants to work at?

IMPLICATIONS FOR TEACHING: A SUMMARY

If we consider carefully the points made so far in Part One we can see clear implications for teachers as curriculum designers and for their classroom teaching. These implications can be summarized as follows.

The teacher must get to know and learn to understand children. She should consider whether she expects too much or too little from children at each stage in their development. Such consideration would include physical, intellectual, and social development of children, and also such things as their motives for learning, how they learn, and factors which might block learning or make learning difficult. She should try to understand that play is important for the growth of the child and be able to make the best use of his natural learning impulses which are evident in his play.

The teacher should be concerned with the thought processes in children. Children's thinking is flexible. Individual children seldom do things the same way and this should be an indication to the teacher of the variety in their patterns of thinking. Should teachers, then, always insist that all children find answers to the same questions or discuss topics in the same way? No child should be hampered by the imposition upon him of routines and procedures which hamper! But the good teacher assists children to develop routines and procedures which help learning to take place.

What is thinking? The word "think" has many meanings and is often very loosely used. In certain cases it means "imagine". When a child daydreams it can be said that he is imagining. Imagining and thinking, however, could be so unlike (if we take the more typical forms of each) that they cannot usefully be used interchangeably. The essence of thinking is that it is controlled by the awareness of a problem and sustained by the attempt to solve it.

On the other hand, educators when talking about a child's *educative thinking* usually refer to it as "meditating or reflecting upon a problem in order to understand the relationships involved." [10] Is this indicating too high a degree of intellectual sophistication for young children? Thinking in this context is a goal-directed activity, the goal being the successful first achievement of a new skill, the gathering of information, the solving of a problem, the presenting of a play, and a countless number of things children strive to do in school.

If teachers take the trouble to understand how children think and what they are naturally capable of doing and want to do at the various stages in their development, they will set more realistic

---

[10] H. J. Klausmeier, *Learning and Human Abilities* (New York: Harper International Student Reprint, 1964), p. 8.

goals for themselves as teachers and help children to set more achievable goals for themselves. The experiences teachers plan for children in order to stimulate learning behavior also will be more in keeping with the needs of the children. Could the structuring of certain experiences for young children of preschool age, in mathematics for example, in the hope that certain concepts will be formed earlier than normal, be largely a waste of time? It could be if the "structuring" is inappropriate and premature. Is not the danger here that all that will be learned is the ability to repeat verbal memorizings without the deeper understandings that go with *real* learning?

The teacher must create the right atmosphere for learning. An atmosphere is an environment which has a "feeling" about it—the kind of thing you sense and know you either like or dislike it. Children very quickly sense the atmosphere of a school and classroom, and seem to know very early whether or not they are happy to be part of it. This colors their reaction to and interaction with the environment.

If we are encouraging learning by discovering, then the atmosphere should be one which promotes the seeking of new knowledge and the exploring of new and interesting situations. It should be an environment full of opportunities for experiences which lead to good learning. There is so much to be discovered in nature, for example, that a child could spend all his time exploring natural science, natural history and natural resources. Similarly, our man-made environment offers a wealth of areas for study.

Experience with a wide selection of materials is essential. A good early childhood room is usually large, with plenty of light, bright colors on the walls and many displays of children's work around the room at the children's eye level. There are small tables and chairs which can be moved to suit the needs of the children's activities. There is a "discovery" table where the children can linger, touching and examining things, thereby discriminating between the properties of these various objects. In one corner there might be a play house where children can indulge in imaginative play where they create and re-create life like situations. The question of physical layout of the classroom will be taken up and developed more fully in Part Three of this book.

A discovery atmosphere encourages independent thought on the part of the learner. The teacher's role is to guide the learner's thinking and to suggest alternative activities for exploration which will add meaning to the discovering process. This indicates the need for careful teacher preparation and teacher-pupil planning. The big question for the teacher, as mentioned earlier, is to know how much guidance is necessary and what kind of guidance is best. The teacher's role is so diverse that she must, if the involvement in learning is to be total, be more than merely adequately prepared. The teacher has to plan, select, and arrange a variety of materials so that related objects can be seen and compared by the learner who in turn selects, arranges, plans and moves on to new learning situations.

Another point to be considered regarding the teacher's role in creating a positive atmosphere for active learning is the attitude of the group, including the teacher, towards mistakes. If teachers and others cannot accept mistakes as a normal part of the learning process then children become tense and anxious, and are thus inhibited from learning by discovery and experiment.

The teacher should stimulate, guide and provide. First, the teacher should stimulate children's thinking by presenting a rich variety of ideas which might arouse their interest either initially, to set their minds moving in a certain direction, or during the learning process when difficulties arise. Children come to a halt in their learning when they cannot see the next step in the process of solving their problem. Without appearing to be over-directive the teacher can suggest a few alternative ideas for the child to explore. With the hesitant child, ideas for exploring might have to be presented in a different way. Of course, the ideal situation is one where the child selects his learning activities from several alternatives provided for him by his understanding teacher who is aware of his interests and his needs. Often with an unimaginative or hesitant child some external stimulus is necessary to arouse his initial interest in a task. The teacher who knows her students well is able to do this in a personal way. New ideas lead to new avenues of seeking information, and by stimulating the imagination of the child an interest is generated and as a result more effective learning occurs. Some hesitant children are quietly thoughtful and sometimes a too hasty idea given by the teacher will interrupt such children's thinking.

Second, some guidance is necessary for *every* growing child. The good teacher is one who knows when and what kind of guidance will be best for a child at any given time. When should the teacher tell the answer to a question? Should she tell at all? How long can a child keep at a difficult task without the help of his teacher? These and similar questions face the teacher each day.

Teachers have a vital role in helping the child develop a liking for learning. The end of school is not the end of learning for any person. The mature member of society is one who continues throughout his life to use his learning skills to solve his problems as they arise in his day-to-day living. Young children are not aware of this. The teacher can hope that, by her example and through the children's participation in a stimulating learning environment, they will enjoy learning and so lay an enduring foundation of learning skills.

Third, it is essential that teachers provide encouragement to children. This encouragement is not the indiscriminate pouring out of praise or the handing out of rewards. Rather it is the way the teacher suggests by her actions that she likes the child for what he is and that she is happy with his attempts to satisfy his drive for knowledge. To such a child the teacher must be a model of all that is worthy in education. This cannot be stressed too much. Teachers are models to children and the good teacher is highly thought of as a friend and confidant.

Teachers can provide the child with encouragement by showing interest in what he is doing; giving advice when needed, or when asked; assisting in organizing activities which will reinforce those already begun by the child; and by encouraging a positive, that is, interested, attitude in the child's activities by the other children in the class.

BIBLIOGRAPHY

Almy, Millie. "Spontaneous Play: An Avenue for Intellectual Development." *The Bulletin of the Institute of Child Study* 28 (November 1966).

Ashton-Warner, Sylvia. *Teacher.* New York: Simon & Schuster, 1963.

Biber, Barbara, et al. *Child Life in School.* New York: E. P. Dutton & Company, 1942.

Combs, A. W., and Snygg, Donald. *Individual Behavior.* New York: Harper ' Row, Publishers, 1959.

Dearden, R. F. *The Philosophy of Primary Education.* London: Routledge and Kegan Paul, 1968.

Fraiberg, Selma. *The Magic Years.* New York: Charles Scribner's & Sons, 1965.

H.M.S.O. *Children and Their Primary Schools.* London: H.M.S.O., 1967.

Holt, John. *How Children Learn.* New York: Pitman Publishing Corporation, 1967.

Hunt, J. McV. *Intelligence and Experience.* New York: The Ronald Press Co., 1961.

Hymes, James L. Jr. *A Child Development Point of View.* Englewood Cliffs, New Jersey: Prentice-Hall, Inc., 1955.

——————. *The Child Under Six.* Englewood Cliffs, New Jersey: Prentice-Hall, Inc., 1963.

——————. *Teaching the Child Under Six,* 2d ed. Columbus, Ohio: Charles E. Merrill Publishing Co., 1974.

Isaacs, Susan. *Childhood and After.* New York: International Universities Press, 1949.

——————. *Intellectual Growth in Young Children.* New York: Schocker Books, 1966.

——————. *The Nursery Years.* New York: Schocken Books, 1968.

Jersild, Arthur T. *Child Psychology,* 6th ed. Englewood Cliffs, New Jersey: Prentice-Hall, Inc., 1968.

Leeper, Sara Hammond, et al. *Good Schools for Young Children.* New York: The Macmillan Co., 1968.

Lowenfeld, Margaret. *Play in Childhood.* New York: John Wiley & Sons, 1967.

Lowenfeld, Viktor, and Lambert, Brittain W. *Creative and Mental Growth,* 5th ed. New York: The Macmillan Co., 1970.

Read, Katherine. *The Nursery School.* Philadelphia: W. B. Saunders, 1966.

Rogers, Vincent R. *Teaching in the British Primary School.* New York: The Macmillan Co., 1971.

Wann, Kenneth, Dorn, M. E.; and Liddle, E. A. *Fostering Intellectual Development in Young Children.* New York: Teachers College Press, 1962.

Weber, Evelyn. *Early Childhood Education; Perspectives on Change.* Worthington, Ohio: Charles A. Jones Publishing Co., 1970.

PART TWO

An Activity-Based Curriculum

Introduction

Part Two aims to provide the teacher with many suggestions on ways to implement an activity, experience-based program of studies. It is divided into two main themes, namely:

1. helping children learn how to communicate
2. helping children discover their environment.

Though these two themes are broad in nature, they encompass many of the "traditional subjects" taught in schools. We have tried to avoid talking about subjects as such for we believe that "subjects" confront the young child with artificial boundaries. After all, subjects are adult in origin and, especially to young children, are frequently barriers to learning. It follows that for the teacher of the young child subjects can be barriers to good teaching. Teachers easily slip into long established practices of teaching reading, mathematics, science, music, etc., as subjects in their own right instead of considering each subject in the broader context of the child's *total* learning.

It should be understood that subjects, as ordered bodies of knowledge, are of growing importance to the educating of the child. As he grows older, and the knowledge he gains and needs to gain becomes more and more complex, he has a need for the orderliness of subjects. But for the young child the broader the areas of curriculum the more suitable they are.

It is a worthy general rule in the education of the young child to let the *main ideas* that are to be introduced and taught by the teacher, and in turn grasped and understood by the child, be few in number and fundamental in purpose. We feel that if this maxim is followed, even in an "open" activity-based curriculum where much of the impetus for learning comes from the child and his interests, then issues are seldom clouded. The child can link his present activities and learning to other things he knows about and has experienced in a variety of situations. If a teacher is not trying too desperately to teach too much at any one time, then the chances are good that what is happening with the child in a planned learning situation will be worthwhile and that much effective, if sometimes unanticipated, learning will take place.

Young children need to learn how to communicate, that is, to be able to tell others of their ideas and experiences. We communicate in many ways—through language, written and oral which includes literature; through drama; music; movement; art. They are, to the young child, interrelated; he does not see them as separate entities.

Young children, as well, need to become familiar with their environment, for learning to live effectively in one's environment is what education is all about. There is for the child no division between his social environment, his scientific environment, nor his mathematical one. Nor should there be a division, for they are part of his everyday life. His environment is one big, bubbling whole which encompasses everything.

If we are to help a child become knowledgeable about his environment, then we need to be ready if a young child displays a natural curiosity about his environment. We need to know so much more about it than what we expect to teach our children if we are to see how it fits together as we hope it will in the child's mind.

A good curriculum is a flexible one. To provide such a flexible curriculum the teacher needs not only to be well informed about what she wants to teach but also to have many ideas about how to go about teaching it. In other words she needs to create a secure, stimulating environment in which communication and exploration are fostered and learning takes place. Let us consider such a learning environment.

The Need for a Secure, Stimulating Environment

It is essential that the child's first experience in nursery school and kindergarten should be a happy one and that he feel secure and comfortable in his new environment. Starting early in a school setting can be a very bewildering experience. The teachers' role is to create an environment of enriching experiences broad enough in scope to meet the individual child's needs, and which at all times will help him adjust to his new learnings.

The development of a child's self-concept has already begun before he comes to school. The teachers' role in this regard is to make the child feel positive about himself, by allowing him time to adjust, time to play, time to experiment, and most of all, time to be a child.

The experiential background of the child is a profoundly influential factor in aiding, or retarding, his adjustment to nursery school and kindergarten settings. If the child feels secure in his relationships at home then he has a better chance of adjusting more easily to school. Unfortunately this is not always the case and teachers cannot rely on each child having such a secure home environment. Whatever his home environment might be when he comes to school, much of a child's subsequent adjustment to his *new* environment depends on the personality of the teacher. If she is sensitive to the growing needs, the experiential background and any special problems that the child faces, then the chances are that the young child's adjustment will be smoother and with fewer traumas than with an insensitive and impatient teacher.

First experiences usually help to form attitudes that are lasting, and the nursery or kindergarten teacher should set a pattern which will aid the development of positive lasting attitudes. It is essential in the early weeks for the teacher to establish routines. Many teachers make the mistake of thinking that freedom in nursery or kindergarten means letting children run wild. Children must develop attitudes of courtesy towards one another, learn to take turns, gain experience at working in groups, and develop feelings of responsibility for materials and equipment. Such routines are a needed part of living together and these early experiences in community living are essential to child development. Training in community living starts as soon as the child enters his new environment. This takes time and teachers should not expect sweeping results quickly. For some children adjusting to routines will be easy because their home environment has already laid the basis for this. But for many children who experience little order in their home life the adjustment will take longer.

Opportunities must be given during free activity periods for children to explore their new environment. It is essential that a variety of experiences be available to the children and that they be allowed to experiment without unnecessary intervention or coercion from the teacher. At the end of each play period a "tidy up time" is necessary, with children helping to put objects back in set places. This is usually a messy business at first but after a few weeks of routine training it can be done in a matter of minutes. It is surprising, too, just how much the children enjoy this part of their daily activities, for it provides them with an outlet for energy and gives them a feeling of security to know that this is their room and everyone has a part in caring for it. As mentioned earlier it is only in a secure, stimulating environment that the child will grow and learn well. The ideal environment should provide opportunities for a variety of experiences that will help the child realize his maximum potential as an individual.

SECTION A

The Development of
Skills of Communication

The Development of Communication through Language: A Product of Growing and Experiencing

It is recognized that from early infancy the child is able in one way or another to communicate his needs. The famished cries of the newly born awakening from a three-hour sleep are demanding and will become frantic if not satisfied quickly. Although such first primitive expressions are not intentional efforts at communicating, most babies learn early that persistent protesting cries will bring a mother to satisfy some need. The desire for mothering manifests itself early in life and often the still fretful baby who has been fed, burped, and changed is communicating some need via its crying, to be picked up, held and cuddled.

The older baby of six months or so is eager to share his reactions to his sensations, for example, the delight he experiences when playing in the bath water. He will communicate this pleasure through facial expressions, happy gurgles and joyful movements. The young baby who squeals with delight on seeing Daddy return from work is also communicating, this time an expressive greeting. Whatever sensation it is, be it an unpleasant or a pleasant one, most young children are capable of communicating their feelings about the sensation long before they can form words. Their facial expressions, gestures and vocalizing are all necessary foundations for a later stage when first words are spoken.

Although young children can adequately express their feelings in a variety of ways long before they are able to verbalize, they will, if they are in an encouraging environment, *begin to feel the need to communicate in words*. This acquiring of a spoken language is one of the great developmental tasks of early childhood.

The acquisition of language is, to many parents, educators, and linguists, one of the most fascinating things to observe. Jersild says that language is a unique accomplishment of human beings and is perhaps the highest form of behavioral development. He believes that the child's early progress in speech is related not only to his cognitive development but also to emotional factors, in particular the attention and affection he receives from adults.[1]

The development of language begins in infancy with the babbling of sounds. At first, the baby responds to the sounds of his mother's voice. At later stages, the child begins to learn sounds by imitating other people and older children he is in contact with. The responses an infant receives in these first attempts to communicate verbally are important, for it is through such responses that the child feels the security and support of some constant adult caretaker—be it mother, father, or another caring individual. The positive responses that a child experiences provides him with an incentive for further repetition and other experimentation.

Much of the young child's early language grows from his play. The very young infant will make sounds as he feels, pulls and manipulates an object. Many parents report that their child's first spontaneous words are associated with some play or with some toy which is a proud possession.

By the age of twelve months many young children have a vocabulary of three, four, or even more words. When the child has learned these few words he uses them in many situations. It is through such practice that he eventually becomes proficient in language. When talking about practice a phrase that comes to mind as an example is "What's this?" Once the young toddler has learned this phrase he is likely for a while to walk around pointing to one thing after another and saying, "What's this?"

Most children have a listening vocabulary which far exceeds their spoken vocabulary—that is, they understand many words which they hear but which they do not yet use. Hence they are often able to follow directions and do things which reflect a considerably higher level of comprehension than might be thought from their still meager speech vocabulary.

Individual children vary greatly in the particular words they first learn and in the rate of acquiring language up to the age of two years. At this age, most children speak in words, phrases and short sentences. However, from about the age of two on, the increase and facility in using language is phenomenal. It is generally agreed that at this stage children develop at a faster rate than any other period in their lives. Huck and Kuhn say the greatest growth in children's language development (that is, not only vocabulary but also language

---

[1] A. T. Jersild, Child Psychology, 6th ed. (Englewood Cliffs, New Jersey: Prentice-Hall, Inc., 1968), p. 415.

structure) is achieved between the ages of two and six.[2] Children learn new words every day and constantly practice them in their play and everyday living. By the time many three-year-olds start nursery school, they are fluent in conversing and are well able to make their needs known.

With this background knowledge of how young children acquire the ability to communicate verbally, how can teachers of young children help them to develop communication skills further? They can help by:

1. recognizing and providing for the fact that each child is different;

2. planning a curriculum of individual as well as common experiences which will give children the opportunity to:

   a. listen effectively;

   b. communicate verbally with one another, and with aides, teachers and other adults;

   c. experience good literature;

   d. become involved in written communication—reading and writing;

   e. participate in music, movement and drama;

   f. communicate through art.

Let us look more closely at each of these points.

EACH CHILD
IS DIFFERENT

When planning curriculum experiences in communication skills the teacher must constantly strive to cater to individual needs, since the teacher will be faced with a group of children who will be very individual in their needs, interests and abilities. Some children will communicate readily and be a delight to talk with, often amazing the teacher with their depth of knowledge of words and their ability to use them. Other children on entering school may be found to have, in one sense, very inadequate communication skills. Often the

---

[2] C. S. Huck and D. Y. Kuhn, *Children's Literature in the Elementary School* (New York: Holt, Rinehart, & Winston, 1968), p. 96.

"culturally disadvantaged" child belongs to this group. The vocabulary these children use at home, while adequate in that situation for the expression of their desires and needs, does not always prepare them for the "school" environment. This need not mean that these young children are inferior in other ways, and indeed, the teacher must try to see that children do not develop feelings of inferiority due to differences in language. Joe L. Frost writes that the empathetic teacher must open the path to verbal communication for the culturally disadvantaged child and accept communication on his terms in the beginning, for he has no other way of communicating.[3]

But the teacher of children of nursery and kindergarten years has a responsibility to extend all of her children's vocabularies irrespective of their previous background in language. She does this according to the individual needs, abilities, and interests of each child, building on the individual's previous experiences, not upon some preconceived normative, socially "acceptable" or standard criterion of language. Therefore she needs to know her children well.

PROVIDING OPPORTUNITIES FOR CHILDREN TO COMMUNICATE VERBALLY EFFECTIVELY

For a child to be able to communicate verbally he must be able to *listen attentively* so that he can hear differences in sounds of words. Some children start school unable to listen discriminately even to sounds, let alone to sequential statements. We, as teachers, can say their skills are poorly developed. Often these children find it difficult to listen to a story. Many of them are used to a high noise level in their homes and have, in fact, learned not to listen.

The following are some games which could be used with children who need practice in developing listening skills.

Dog and the Bone

Children sit in a small circle. One child is chosen to be the puppy who, with eyes closed, guards the bone. Individual children creep up to take his bone. If the "puppy" hears them he wakes up and barks. Many variations are possible to maintain the children's interest—for example, a cat and a saucer of milk.

---

[3] Joe L. Frost, "What It Takes to Make a Difference," *Grade Teacher* reprint (1966), p. 12.

Who Am I?

Children sit with eyes closed while the teacher taps a child on the head, who then says, "Who am I?" The group guesses who it is.

Listening to Sounds Outside

Children listen and tell the group of the sounds they can hear outside the classroom.

Listening to Sounds Inside the Room

Children close their eyes and listen for sounds inside the room— teacher writing on the chalkboard, opening and closing a book, etc. Once the game is understood, children may take turns at making sounds.

What Am I?

Teacher makes the sound of a familiar object and the children identify it—e.g., a car. Children take turns in making sounds of familiar objects or activities.

What Animal Am I?

Teacher initially makes the sound of an animal and children identify it. Then individual children may take turns while others identify it.

What Did I Tap?

Start with three percussion instruments placed in the center of a small group of children. The children close their eyes while someone taps an instrument. The children try to identify the instrument. Gradually increase the number of instruments used.

What Did I Shake?

Have two identical containers, one with chalk in it and the other one with stones. The children must identify the sounds. Gradually increase the number of containers used and vary the contents.

Clapping Rhythms

The teacher claps a simple rhythm and asks an individual child to clap it back. Children may take turns at clapping a rhythm.

Tape Recording

Tape record the teacher's and childrens' voices. Let the children listen and identify the voices.

Listening to Recordings

Listen to recordings and identify the sounds of, for example, an airplane, ambulance.

In order to develop verbally, children not only must have many opportunities for hearing language spoken, but they must also have opportunities for communicating with other children and with adults. Children coming from an enriched home environment usually have developed considerable facility in using language by the time they enter nursery school. Such children will often talk readily and contribute in group discussions. These children, however, also need to have many opportunities for using language so that they are stimulated and challenged to extend themselves further.

Other children, often many children, on entering school, are found to talk less readily and to have a variety of language problems. They need very individualized help. Often these children will be silent and withdrawn in large group discussions. They need more individual and small group work to help them overcome their extreme shyness.

The teacher has to provide many experiences which will give all children the opportunity to talk together and to acquire new expressions of language. Each day many spontaneous experiences will develop which the teacher will use to extend the children's language. But she must have sound, well-planned objectives which she will implement to achieve her communication goals with most of her children. A great deal of language experiences will grow out of centers of interest. Such centers begin with a topic which is of such intense interest to the children that the work of the class, group, or individual, may center around it for a day, week, two weeks, a month, or in some instances, even longer.

The following list suggests experiences to be used in developing verbal communication.

1. Provide for centers of interest to grow out of topics introduced by the teacher. Such a provision might be through developing a *central theme* in a classroom—e.g., animals we have as pets, colors that are gay.

2. Encourage the children to talk about the things arising out of their centers of interest which they have made in creative periods. These constructions should be linked with the teacher's central theme planning.

3. Introduce a *touch table* where objects of varying texture are displayed. This table should be in a place accessible to the children so they can linger, touch and talk about the objects placed on the table. Objects could include: pine cone, piece of cotton wool, piece of velvet material, corduroy, some sand paper, and plastic. The children should be encouraged to talk about the texture of these objects using words such as soft, rough, smooth, hard, prickly, etc. Many new words can be introduced this way.

4. Introduce other *sensory experiences* where the children can smell and sometimes taste. In this way sensory perception can be developed. This development could be aided by enjoyable cooking experiences. For example: popping pop-corn, making cup cakes, making pan cakes, making cookies. These kinds of experiences, if handled well by the teacher, provide opportunities for all sorts of incidental language teaching and can stimulate all the senses—seeing, hearing, smelling and tasting. It should be noted once again cooking experiences should evolve out of the centers of interest whenever possible and be related to the on-going experiences of the classroom themes.

5. Establish a *nature area* in the room where flowers, leaves and other specimens of *current interest* are collected. The children should be encouraged to bring to school things to add to this nature area. Informal discussions should be held about these objects. Children should also be encouraged to find with the teacher any additional information about simple experiments, such as rate of growth of things alive, the "hardness" of various rocks, etc.

6. Develop an outside garden, if it is at all possible, where seeds and plants may be planted and cared for. Children usually watch carefully and are very excited when some change in growth has occurred. This will usually stimulate lively discussions and provide many opportunities for the introduction of new language. In addition to outside gardening, much can be done with indoor planting in pots. Young children readily

assume responsibility for caring for pot plants and sharing observations about growth, flowers, leaves, perfume.

7. Go on *nature walks* in the school ground and immediate surroundings. These walks can stimulate discussions about flowers, leaves, trees, birds, weather and seasonal changes. Such walks can occur frequently and do not require all the organizational planning needed for longer bus trips.

8. Go on planned *field trips* which are related to the current classroom central themes, such as fire station, zoo, farm.

9. Play games such as "Which toy is missing?" Begin this game by placing three interesting toys in the center of a small group of children. The children close their eyes while another child quickly removes and hides a toy. The group must guess which toy is missing. The number of toys used should be gradually increased. This game can also be linked with the centers of interest and be played with any other interesting objects.

PROVIDING OPPORTUNITIES TO BECOME INVOLVED WITH WRITTEN COMMUNICATION

Literature

Literature plays a very important part in helping children develop the skills of communication. It can not, however, be taken for granted that it is an easy skill to develop. In recent times attention has been focused on the inability of many young children to enjoy literature. The "culturally disadvantaged" have been singled out in this particular regard. We cannot say that these children do not enjoy literature but rather we should look upon it as a problem of language communication. If children cannot understand the language of a particular story, then they are not going to enjoy it. This makes careful selection of first stories essential for children facing such language problems.

Presenting literature to children should be an enjoyable experience for both children and teachers. It is a time when a common bond between teacher and child is developed and tensions and fears disappear. In literature a child can escape into another world. Children often have been heard at the end of a story to say spontaneously, "Read it again." This can be an indication that the story was a good choice for the age level of those children and also that it was well presented by the teacher. Children seldom tire of hearing favorite stories read again and again. Often, too, the popular stories have an element of repetition in them and children are able to join in with the narrator, thus becoming even more involved.

Children should have many opportunities for listening to literature. A good number of children come to school from an environment which has not provided experiences in literature. Not only those called by convention the "culturally disadvantaged" are included here. Many parents, unfortunately, overlook the fact that children can appreciate literature at a very early age. Children, on entering school, should be exposed to books as soon as possible and have the opportunity of hearing stories from books that are within their level of understanding and vocabulary.

DEVELOPING AN INTEREST IN STORY BOOKS

The teacher needs to provide many opportunities for the child to discover books for himself. The library reading corner must be attractive, with books in accessible places. During "free activity" periods each day the child should be able to go to the library corner and browse through books. The teacher, however, should never use coercion in trying to interest a child in story books, and also should not forget that children vary greatly in their interests. Some of the more mature children will be stimulated to go and explore books immediately. For others it may take longer. *Much will depend on the amount of interest that the teacher arouses when she presents books during story times.* If the child enjoys a story then it is likely that he will want to go and explore the book for himself.

THE TEACHER AS A STORYTELLER

The teacher should be an excellent storyteller and story reader, capable of holding the children spellbound. The classroom arrangement plays a significant role in the presentation of a story. It is important for the teacher of young children to have the children sitting close to her when she reads or tells a story. This arrangement develops a bond between teacher and children—the storyteller and the listeners. Sitting near the teacher, children are better able to see the story book if one is being used and the teacher does not need to use volume other than her normal voice.

Sometimes the whole class may be listening to a story and at other times it may just be a group of children who, during free activity time, have asked the teacher to read them a story. The teacher should seldom need to interrupt a story to discipline a child. If the attention of a child wanders, then the story is either not suitable or the teacher is not presenting it in a convincing way. A teacher who knows the interest level of her class and knows how to present a story can hold the listening group in rapt attention.

The teacher should allow children to show their preferences for certain story books by encouraging them to select a book. "It is Peter's turn to choose a story today." If the teacher wants to introduce a new story, then it can be her turn.

DEVELOPING AN INTEREST IN PICTURES

Illustrations in the better children's books today are an integral part of the story and the child therefore needs to be able to interpret pictures. This is especially true of picture books. Huck and Kuhn say,

> A picture book is a book in which the pictures are designed to be an integral part of the text. The fusion of both pictures and text is essential for the unity of presentation.[4]

In order to develop this skill of fusing story and illustrations the teacher will need to provide experiences where the children see interesting pictures and attempt to gain meaning from them. She could provide short informal "picture talks" where a large picture which is of some special interest to the children at that particular time is displayed, and the children are encouraged to make spontaneous comments about it. Another way of developing this skill is to show the story book pictures again after the story has been read.

In general if the teacher understands the needs of individual children—their experiential background, interest levels, and specific problems such as their level of language development or lack of listening skills—then she has a background of information which will aid her in successfully teaching literature. It is important that she knows the best ways to present stories and story books to children, although there can be no prescribed way of telling stories, for in good storytelling a personal and intimate bond develops between teller and listener. Literature should provide the child with joy and pleasure and should satisfy "his craving for hearing the new, the old, the unusual, the exciting."

---

[4] Huck and Kuhn, p. 108.

Reading

The age-old controversy about when to begin the teaching of reading still is with us today. On one side of the argument we have educators stressing the need to consider the child's all-round development before introducing him to formal reading. On the other side we see preschool programs which introduce formal reading early in the program in the belief that all or most children can be taught to read at a very early age.

It is unfortunate that in recent years so much publicity has been given to reading failure. Many school principals, class teachers, reading specialists and parents have become over anxious about the teaching of reading. The undue emphasis placed on reading has the unfortunate result of making it an isolated subject in the curriculum. Children have become reading "failures" even in the kindergarten and have been termed "non-readers" at a very early age. Indeed, the reputation of teachers and principals, and of the very school systems themselves, tends greatly to stand or fall by how favorably the children measure on standardized national reading tests.

Research on the teaching of reading is very extensive and covers all facets of reading: when to begin formal reading, what method to use, what text to use, specific reading disabilities, and so on. Certain general directives emerge from all this research, namely, that:

1. There is no one best time for all children to begin formal reading. Neither chronological nor mental age is of itself a reliable indicator of readiness to profit from formal reading instruction.

2. Readiness for reading rests on a number of factors, namely:
   The child's language development
   His background of experiences
   His physical development
   His social development
   His emotional development
   His intellectual development
   His desire to want to learn to read
   The opportunities he has to learn how to read.

3. There is no one current method for beginning the teaching of reading which is more successful than any one other. Individual children respond differently and therefore need to have

their reading program planned to suit their individual learning style. One child may respond quickly and progress rapidly when learning, for example, by a whole word/look and say approach. Another child may need to begin reading with a purely phonic approach.

THE PLACE OF READING IN
THE CURRICULUM OF NURSERY SCHOOLS

It is the opinion of the writers that the teaching of formal reading has very little, if any, place in a nursery school for three-and four-year-olds. Very few three-and four-year-olds are ready to profit from the formal teaching of reading. There is no doubt that many children of this age can be taught to read, but the gains achieved in time and fluency (ability) are questionable. Usually the methods used in such early instruction are very formalized and rigid and can result in the children becoming uninterested in reading rather than developing into avid readers.

Research also shows that it is detrimental to push young children during the initial stages of learning to read, for what could be the resulting sense of failure gets the children off to a bad start with their reading. If teachers have a thorough understanding of the concept of *readiness* they will avoid pressuring children into beginning formal reading too soon. Readers should refer to Part One of this book where *readiness* has been more fully discussed.

One of the main functions of the nursery school should be to provide a rich environment, free from pressures and frustrations, which will lay the basis for those skills the child will later use when he does begin reading.

Some ways in which the nursery school teacher can provide the basis for later development of reading skills are by:

1. helping the child to become adjusted to nursery school.
2. broadening the child's background of experiences.
3. helping the child develop socially—offering opportunities for play with other individuals and group participation.
4. helping the child develop his skill at oral communication.
5. providing activities which will aid motor coordination.
6. providing experiences which will help the child develop his skill at auditory and visual discrimination and develop his other senses.

7. helping the child develop a love for books and an interest in print.

Let us look more closely at each of these points.

1. *Helping the child become adjusted to nursery school.* This point has been developed more fully earlier in this chapter and its importance cannot be overstated. If the child feels happy and secure he will be able to enter willingly into experiences in the planned curriculum which lay the basis for reading.

2. *Broadening the child's background of experiences.* Fred Schonell, discussing factors which underlie reading ability, argued for a program of activities which would bridge the gap between home and school. Such a program would enable children to assimilate vocabulary and ideas that they would later use in their reading.[5]

   Most nursery school teachers are aware of the value of expanding the child's breadth of experiences as a prerequisite for later success in reading. These experiences will generally arise out of the central theme.[6]

3. *Helping the child to develop socially.* It is through contact with other children and his teachers that the child acquires acceptable social behavior. In his interaction with other children he learns to share willingly, to take turns and to experience the spontaneous joy of playing with other children of his age. Readers should refer to Part One of this book and the section which talks about *play*.

   In the part of the nursery school classroom set aside for the doll's house (or home corner), it is fascinating to observe the play of young children. Through their play and interests new levels of understanding are achieved and oppressive fears may be played out in fantasy play. For example, the three-year-olds will play over and over again a visit to the doctor or some other painful experience.

   A warning should be made here. With the introduction to the classroom of paraprofessionals and other helpers, there

---

[5] Fred J. Schonell, *Psychology of Teaching Reading* (New York: Philosophical Library, 1961), p. 49.

[6] The term *central theme* refers to a method of planning those situations which the teacher presents to her children every day. It is based on the idea that as much *integration* of areas of learning that can be done should be done.

is a danger of too close supervision of imaginative play. Intrusions by "helpful" adults often will stifle imaginative play. It is important for children to feel sometimes that they are alone and free from adult interference.

Over a period of time the nursery school child will usually display growth in self-confidence, in himself, with his peer group and with his teacher. All this is necessary for future success in reading.

4. *Helping the child develop his skills at oral communications.* All of the experiences in developing communication skills arising out of the planned central themes and the spontaneous centers of interest can be used for preparing the child for reading. The verbal communication which goes on between teacher and child, and between child and child develops skills which create the functional language background essential for success in reading. Before a child is required to learn to read he must be able to *talk* fluently. The nursery school can provide for much oral communicating.

5. *Providing opportunities which will aid motor coordination.* It should be remembered that outdoor experiences are just as essential as indoor play to the development of motor coordination. In the outdoor play period the teacher should aim to vary the equipment used so that children will have many opportunities to promote large muscle development and muscular coordination. There are some pieces of outdoor play equipment which remain fixed such as the steel jungle gyms and swings, but to these there should be added other equipment of a "changing" kind. Jumping boards, for example, can be set up in differing arrangements and used for balancing or jumping skills. Hoops can be used for running, jumping and free play. Large balls can be used for rolling and throwing. Ropes can be added to the jungle gyms in varying arrangements.

The connection between such vigorous outdoor activities and the quite delicate motor skills required for reading may not at first sight seem to be clear. But the development of coordination of the larger muscles must precede that of the smaller muscles. It is, indeed, indispensable.

6. *Providing experiences which will help auditory, visual, and sensory discrimination.* In the nursery school the development of aural and visual skills should be done in a relaxed, informal

way. The following are examples of suitable experiences for young children which will aid:

A. *Visual Discrimination*

(1) Displays can be developed arising out of centers of interest. For example, displays of colored objects which provide children with many opportunities for discovering likenesses and differences in color, shape, size, texture and even aroma. These displays usually center at first on one or two colors and children collect many and varied objects of these colors. Scrap material

Children Sorting, Matching, and Classifying Objects

is a good source for this kind of activity. Such displays usually create sustained interest by the children.

(2) Collections of leaves, flowers, berries, shells, and other natural phenomena will afford experiences for visual discrimination. Children can observe very quickly the

leaves that are the same, which ones are tiny and which are large, which are shiny and which are less shiny and so on. After some initial direction by the teacher many children will be capable of making very fine discriminations between objects.

(3) Nature walks where children look for specific things afford learning experiences in visual discrimination.

B. *Aural Discrimination*

(1) Many of the listening games mentioned on pages 38 and 39 are suitable for nursery school children but it should be stressed again that these games should be played only with small groups of children.

(2) Percussion band work will help develop aural discrimination. When children become familiar with percussion instruments, they will be able to recognize the individual instruments by sound. Tapping back simple rhythms from memory is also good aural training.

(3) Listening to well chosen recordings of songs, sounds, and stories will also aid aural discrimination.

(4) Building up a repertoire of well selected songs which are within the comprehension of the children and are known and enjoyed by them is an essential part of the nursery school curriculum. Much aural training is achieved by utilizing the repertoire in everyday activities.

C. *Other Sensory Development*

Experiences for the development of other senses are closely tied in with those listed for visual and aural development. Specific activities to develop the other senses include:

(1) Introduction of a "touch table" (as mentioned on page 41) containing objects of differing texture; for example, pine cone, cotton, pieces of velvet fabric, leaves, glass. There are many available examples of objects of differing textures. These should be collected and used.

(2) Feeling Bag: a fabric bag with different textured objects placed in it helps children to become aware of texture by touch. (Children identify objects by feeling them in the bag.)

(3) Asking a child to identify an object by touch when it is dropped into his hands which are held behind his back.

(4) Introduction of a variety of goods which have distinct odors—onions, spices, suitable pieces of fruit and vegetables.

7. *Helping the child develop a love for books and an interest in print.* Some children enter nursery school having heard stories at home and are already eager to listen to stories and to explore books for themselves. Other children are not so fortunate and do not experience story books before entering nursery school.

It is essential that in the nursery school environment there be a quiet place where children have access to books and are able to sit down to look at them undisturbed. For this reason it is important to place the "book area" away from busy traffic. Furthermore, the book corner should always look inviting and the books be changed frequently.

TEACHING READING IN THE KINDERGARTEN

When discussing the teaching of reading in the kindergarten there are certain factors which must be considered, namely:

1. children are individually different with regard to background in reading readiness and motivation to want to read;

2. the teacher is responsible for the development of a stimulating environment which will arouse in the child the desire to learn to read;

3. the teacher needs to be aware of the many incidental ways of teaching reading in the kindergarten;

4. the teacher needs a vast ready repertoire of ideas, games, activities and aids to make early reading attempts meaningful and stimulating to the child.

Let us consider these four factors in more detail.

1. *Individual differences with regard to reading.* Some children on entering kindergarten are eager and ready to make their own story books and learn to "read". Others have not yet reached the "what does it say?" stage and will often be lacking

in the early skills necessary for success in reading. The old and inescapable problem of individual differences discussed in Part One comes to the fore again, and allowances for individual differences in kindergarten are as crucial in reading as they are in any other skill development. The bright five-year-old, eager to get at books, who spends weeks working at visual discrimination exercises because he has been told to do so by his teacher will soon become bored and frustrated. His subsequent lack of interest will work against his reading development. We have, in addition, all heard of the parent who has to make perhaps five or six trips to the school in the hope of convincing someone, especially her child's teacher, that Suzy is reading already. Unfortunately, these visits may be fruitless and Suzy continues with the reading readiness ditto sheets and other pointless (for Suzy) readiness exercises for six months. This all demonstrates the need for a curriculum which will allow children who are ready to read—to read! Meanwhile other children who need to develop the skills necessary for future success in reading should be helped by the teacher to develop those skills. In other words a *whole* class should not be working at any one level of reading at any one time, including "reading readiness" exercises. And indeed they cannot effectively do so.

2. *The teacher needs to develop a stimulating environment which will arouse in children the desire to learn to read.* A child is likely to have much more difficulty in learning to read if his environment, at home and at school, is not pervaded by books and other printed materials. Too often in the past reading in the kindergarten has been taught at a set time each day when children worked at pre-reading exercises and later at reading books, after which the books and other materials were put away. Little wonder over the years that reading achievements have been poor.

One reading method which creates great interest in read-ing in a stimulating yet individual way is what is called the *Language Experience Approach.* This approach to reading is not new; its growth can be traced back to the 1920's when "activity centered" ideas became popular. With this approach the children must first be involved in some meaningful experi-ence. It could be a trip to a farm, an exciting person who visited the classroom, some child's pet which is "visiting" the class for the day, or a party. Reading experiences grow out of the things that the children do. The teacher uses the actual language of the children to construct in chart, story, or diary

**Helping the Development of Relationships between
Children Can Also Help the Development of Language**

form the experiences the children have had. Language experience can be a group experience with individual children con-
tributing to a story, or it can be an individual child's story.

When beginning language experience work, it is essential
that the teacher use as nearly as possible the language of
the children, keeping changes to an absolute minimum as
this is the language that the children will in turn "read". In
these early stages changing the children's language (for example, the grammatical structure of their tenses) effects no long
lasting result and will often destroy language spontaneity. Such
changes may inhibit the self-confidence of the children and
make them reluctant to contribute orally.

Initial language experience work with kindergarten in
order to make the early stages of recognition easier should
be limited to reasonably short sentences which are stimulating
and meaningful. The sentences should be interrelated with
some other creative work such as art. For example, after a
visit to a zoo children could have their stories written on a
large mural which in turn would be illustrated in appropriate
media—paint, torn paper, scrap material, etc. In this way reading is not treated as an isolated subject. It should, in fact,
permeate all areas of the kindergarten curriculum.

Fishes flip their fins and swim

A Display of Children's Work Illustrating
the Language Experience Approach

Language experience charts, projects, stories and other work should be displayed as attractively and prominently as possible. When children see their own words in printed form they begin to understand fairly quickly that printed symbols stand for something. There is no better way of getting children to realize this, or of stimulating their own desires to read.

3. *The teacher needs to be aware of the many incidental ways of teaching reading in the kindergarten.* There are many incidental ways of beginning the teaching of reading rather than by introducing first primers. Many kindergarten teachers are able to start children reading with incidental activities. The following is a list of such incidental reading activities suitable for kindergarten.

A. *Recognition of names*

This can be started early in the year. The only material required is a set of the children's names written in manuscript on cards. Activities which help children to learn their names include:

(1) Find your name when you first enter the classroom in the morning and place it on a board, or in a bag, or by an activity area where you want to work.

(2) Teacher flashes the children's names and children respond to:
"Stand when you see your name."
"Clap when you see your name."
"Hop to the door when you see your name."

(3) A few children place their names on a board. They close their eyes while a child removes a name and then asks "Which name is missing?"

(4) Teacher writes the children's names on all their work during the day.

B. *Labelling objects in the classroom and labelling activity areas*

For example:

Our nature table

Block corner

Library corner

Playhouse

FIGURE ONE

It is important that the teacher do this labelling work *with* the children rather than labelling areas of the room before the children begin school.

Any labelling activity should be done in a stimulating, meaningful way with the children active participants in the experience.

C.   *Teacher displays on flash cards sentences for certain activities*

    For example:

It is lunch time

It is circle time

FIGURE TWO

D.   *Introduction of verb cards:*

    For example:

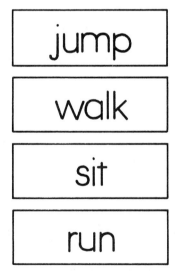

FIGURE THREE

Small group flash card games can be played to facilitate the learning of these verbs. Suitable games include:

(1) Throwing a bean bag on to the flash cards placed on the floor.

(2) *Postman game.* The postman delivers the flash card "letters" (words) while the children close their eyes. On signal all wake up and read their "letters".

(3) *Fishing game.* Verbs are written on cards which are cut to resemble fish. Paper clips are attached to the fish which are placed in a "pond" (carton).
Using a rod with a small magnet attached children "fish out" the cards.

E. *Labelling work in the centers of interest*

For example a center of interest developed around zoo animals could include names of animals and parts of the zoo which the children had made, perhaps in the sand tray.

F. *Labelling objects on the nature table*

Current objects on the nature table can be labelled and the children's stories about science recorded. Remember that the "stories" should be:

> # The sweet potato is growing roots

FIGURE FOUR

G. *Current cooking recipes*

Teacher writes on large pieces of paper the recipes of any current cooking activities. These recipes should be displayed and used again when the activity is repeated with a new group of children.

4. *The teacher needs a vast ready repertoire of ideas, games, activities and aids* to make early reading attempts meaningful and stimulating to the child. For example:

A. *Flash card games*

The following are some flash card games suitable for introducing new vocabulary and revising known words.

(1) *Spin Knife, Spin.* Flash cards are placed in a small circle. A child spins a knife in the center of the circle and reads the word it stops at.

(2) *Lucky Dip.* Flash cards are placed in a deep box. A child comes to the box and dips for a card.
The children chant: "Have a lucky dip today, and see what luck will come your way."

Five and Six Year Olds Engaging in Group Language Activity

(3) *The Sentry.* A child is chosen to be the sentry guarding a castle. A second child marches up.
Sentry: Stop!
Child: May I come in?

Sentry: If you know the pass card.
Child: (Looks at the card and answers.)
Sentry: Pass! (If the right answer is given.)

(4) *Pass the Card.*   Children sit in a small circle, pass cards, and say: "Pass, pass, pass the cards." On a signal the children with cards stand up and read them.

(5) *Balloons.*   Circles representing balloons into which words are printed are drawn on the blackboard. Individual children read the words and then erase them if correct.

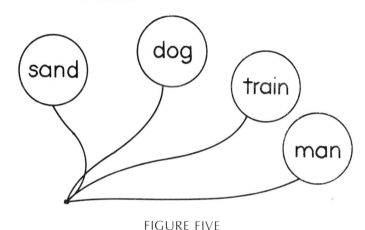

FIGURE FIVE

FIGURE SIX

(6) *Stepping Stones.*   Words are written on cards and placed on the floor in the manner of stepping stones. Individual children read the cards and if correct continue to "home base".

(7) *Tick-tack-toe.*   Using a long pointer a child points to a set of flash cards and says:

"Tick-tack-toe
Here I go.
Where I stop
I do not know."
The child picks up the last card pointed to and reads
it. The order of cards is changed for the next turn.

(8) *Relay Race.* Small groups of children form two
teams. A leader is chosen for each team and a pile
of flash cards for each team is placed faced down
on the floor near each team leader. On a signal
children race up, read the card and run back to their
team. Team leaders write the score on the chalkboard. The team with the most points is the winner.

(9) *Dice Game.* Reading words can be written in chalk
on a large wooden dice. Children take turns at rolling
the dice and reading the words which come up.

(10) *Bowling.* A set of bowling pins can be made out
of plastic bottles with word flash cards attached by
large paper clips to the neck of the bottle. The children bowl a ball, try to knock down the bottles, and
say the words on the bottles which remain standing.

B.   *Individual work cards.*

Teachers should make individual sets of work cards containing relevant vocabulary. For example:

(1) *Read and Draw Cards*

Read and draw
A red car
A fat man
A black dog
A big ship

FIGURE SEVEN

(2) *Read and Make Cards.* For a read and make activity children can use clay, other modelling media, colored paper and scrap material.

Read and make
A zoo with
5 elephants
3 tigers
2 camels

FIGURE EIGHT

(3) *Reading Puzzles.*

I am black
I have 4 legs
I drink milk
I say "meow"
What am I ?
Draw me

FIGURE NINE

(4) *Read and Do Cards.*   Teacher flashes a card and writes a child's name on the blackboard:

Run to the door.	John
Skip to the window.	Mary
Hop to the table.	Janet

FIGURE TEN

(5) *Word Matching Cards.*   Individual sets of word matching cards can be made containing relevant vocabulary. For example:

FIGURE ELEVEN

Small words for matching can be placed in envelopes glued to the back of the card.

(6) *Activities to develop left to right eye movement.*   For example:

FIGURE TWELVE

Material required: sets of individual cards and round curtain rings. The children put a curtain ring on the object which is different. The sets of cards can be designed to cover all types of likenesses and differences and be graded according to the degree of difficulty.

C. *Picture interpretation experiences.*

Many initial reading books (primers) place emphasis on picture interpretation. The children associate a picture with a printed word. In order for children to be able to do this activity they need experience in talking about pictures and gaining meaning from them. Teachers need to collect large, interesting pictures and mount them on cardboard for strength and durability. They can then be used for picture interpretation activities. This is one very obvious place where language development permeates all aspects of the curriculum.

Writing

Most four- and five-year-old children are not capable of the coordination and control required in the "simple" act of writing. For this reason any formal instruction in writing in nursery school is undesirable. This is also true for most kindergarten children. Early attempts to introduce formal writing in kindergarten usually result in the child being frustrated.

Rather, the whole emphasis in nursery school and kindergarten should be on experiences and activities which will lay the basis for writing at a later time. The time, however, will depend on the individual development of each child. Art experiences discussed later in Part Two on page 94 help develop the muscular coordination needed for writing. In addition there are other sensory experiences such as the following which are suitable for young children. They could also be termed essential prerequisites to the first formal steps in learning to write in that they aid sensory discrimination and large muscle development.

WATER PLAY

For the young child the value of water play cannot be overemphasized. Here the sense of touch, the developing ability and refining of muscular coordination (such as when the child pours water from container to container) help the child develop those skills which he will later use when writing. The soothing feel of the water; the joy of communicating with another while playing with water; the vast amount of incidental learning which takes place through pouring and measuring; the dawning realization that some objects float, some sink—all make water play an essential experience to be included in the school curriculum. Very often it is through water play that the shyer child will lose some of his inhibitions and interact with his peers. For maximum benefit water play needs to be limited to small groups.

Aids for use in water play:

  Plastic beakers of varying sizes
  Detergent bottles, shampoo bottles
  Food coloring (for children can watch the water change color)
  Soap solution, bubble pipes, or straws
  Sponges
  Rubber balls
  Cooking utensils from the play house
  Lightweight egg beater (for use with water and soap)
  Boats
  Objects that float or sink.

SAND BOX PLAY

Playing with sand is another excellent sensory experience which aids muscular coordination. In summer sand play can be linked with water play, for children will almost always seek out water to mix with sand. If the sand box is an out-of-doors one, it is essential to keep it covered when not in use. The sand box area should look attractive and inviting and the sand toys should be varied to stimulate interest.

The use of sand indoors is somewhat limited when compared to out-of-doors sand play, but nevertheless a sand tray can be used constructively inside. Sifting, pouring, measuring experiences can be done inside and the sand tray can lend itself to display purposes.

Aids for sand box play:

  Sifters (holes in the bottom of a can, or a frame around a piece
    of wire mesh makes a functional sifter)
  Funnels

A Child at Sand Play
A Teacher Should Always Supervise Such Play

A tray of accessory toys such as plastic pitchers, tin cans, of
    all sizes, small buckets, spades, wooden spoons, tubs
Vegetable strainers
Tea strainers

BLOCK PLAY

Block play provides a means of creative expression for young children
as well as enhancing muscular control and development. Young
children are interested in blocks from early infancy when they handle
and roll blocks covered with cloth. This interest does not wane and
young children in nursery and kindergartens will remain absorbed
for long periods playing very creatively with blocks. It is essential
that a large space be planned for the block area.

Often the children will construct something arising from the
center of interest. This construction should be left for a time until
the interest wanes. Large empty milk cartons make practical blocks

A Child at Block Play

if cleaned and taped across the opening. The cartons will resemble brick blocks if covered with paper torn and glued to them.

ACTIVITIES USING WOOD

Woodworking is a particularly enjoyable experience for young children. It is a means of self-expression as well as for the development of muscular skill and coordination. It is an activity, however, which requires close supervision and should be included in the curriculum only if there is a low pupil/teacher ratio which will allow for adequate supervision. Unless closely supervised, children can injure themselves with equipment and are often likely to experience frustration if there is not an adult at hand to help them with construction. Woodworking could, however, be the kind of activity where a father, mother, grandparent, or other available adult could be available for an hour or so on certain days to provide the necessary supervision.

It should be remembered that woodworking is not restricted only to boys. In addition, it should be remembered that the young four- and five-year-olds are not capable of "real" construction (i.e., construction in a building or carpentry sense) using carpentry tools and timber. Although most children of this age can use a hammer and drive a nail, other carpentry tools are more difficult for the young child. The temptation is for the "supervising adult," the teacher, parent, aide, to do the construction themselves. When this happens the activity is of questionable value for the children.

If the classroom provides for woodworking, then equipment should be the best available if children are to use it functionally, since inferior equipment is both dangerous and frustrating to the children attempting to use it. Furthermore, equipment should be introduced gradually. Initially the children could handle small pieces of scrap wood, gluing together objects and arrangements, which can be painted with poster paint. From this beginning activity, nails and a hammer for joining wood can be introduced, and finally a saw. Sawing timber not only can be dangerous for young children, but often is very frustrating as it requires muscular strength which they do not yet have. To aid in sawing activities "G" clamps, or better still a vise attached to a work bench, is really essential. These tools will hold the timber to a bench or table while the children manipulate the saw. Other tools from the list included here can be introduced as needed. It should be remembered that the number of children working with wood at any one time should be limited to two or three.

Woodwork equipment:

> Suitable work bench with a vise on either side
> Hammers (wooden handle with claw)
> Nails (flat-head—1½" and 2")
> Supply of soft woods (pines, poplar)
> Sand paper (medium and coarse)
> Plane
> Brace and bit
> Saws (small size cross-cut)
> Screwdrivers (6" to 8")
> Carpenters' pencils

TOYS WHICH ARE DESIGNED TO AID MANIPULATIVE SKILLS

There are available today many commercially produced toys and games which purport to be educational in design and purpose. Teachers should examine these carefully before including them in classroom equipment. While many of these products are excellent, others are quite unsuitable, either having little appeal to children or requiring small muscular manipulation of which the young child is not capable.

In addition to commercially produced equipment there are other manipulative objects which can be found in the home or other available sources. The following equipment, if selected wisely, can be useful in developing manipulative skills:

Jigsaw puzzles
Large beads with laces for threading
Larger varieties of snap blocks
Larger variety of Tinker Toys
Old fashioned door locks with handles
Old clocks which will wind up
Plastic bottles with screw tops
Large stapling machines
Large spools.

OTHER SENSORY EXPERIENCES

Included here would be provision for those experiences outlined in pages 40-42. In addition cooking experiences which are interrelated with the central theme and centers of interest should be provided. Such experiences should be well planned, and the actual mixing of recipes should involve small groups of children rather than the whole class. A list of recipes is given in Appendix B.

BIBLIOGRAPHY

Books

Arbuthnot, May H. *Children and Books*. Chicago: Scott, Foresman & Co., 1964.

Gans, Roma; Stendler, Celia; and Almy, Millie. *Teaching Young Children*. Yonkers-on-Hudson: World Book Company, 1952.

Huck, C. S., and Kuhn, D. Y. *Children's Literature in the Elementary School*. New York: Holt, Rinehart & Winston, 1968.

Hymes, James L. *Teaching the Child Under Six*, 2d ed. Columbus Ohio: Charles E. Merrill Publishing Company, 1974.

Jersild, Arthur T. *Child Psychology*, 6th ed. Englewood Cliffs, New Jersey: Prentice Hall, Inc., 1968.

Leeper, Sarah H.; Dales, Ruth; Skipper, Dora; and Witherspoon, Ralph. *Good Schools for Young Children*. New York: The Macmillan Co., 1968.

Plowden, Lady B. "The Plowden Report" in *Children and Their Primary School*. London: H.M.S.O., 1966.

Rogers, Vincent R. *Teaching in the British Primary School*. London: The Macmillan Company, 1970, Chapter 5.

Schonell, Fred J. *Psychology of Teaching Reading*. New York: Philosophical Library, 1961.

Articles

Church, Joseph, "Language in Childhood." *Childhood Education* (September 1962): 19.

Huck, Charlotte S. "Literature's Role in Language Development." *Childhood Education* (November 1965): 147-50.

Margolin, Edythe. "Conservation of Self Expression and Aesthetic Sensitivity in Young Children." *Young Children* (January 1968): 155-60.

Rich, Dorothy. "Spurring Language Creativity in Young Children." *Young Children* (January 1968): 175-77.

Pamphlets

Association for Childhood Education International. "Good and Inexpensive Books for Children." Washington D.C.: A.C.E.I., 1972.

Hymes, James L. "Teacher Listen. The Children Speak." New York: National Association for Mental Health, 1949.

CHAPTER TWO

The Development of Communication through Music, Movement, and Drama

For young children music, movement and drama are so interrelated that it is unwise to attempt to separate them. We should not, therefore, talk about a "music program" or a "dance program" or a "drama program" as if each was a separate strand in a subject-oriented curriculum. It is unwise, too, to become so technical in our approach to each of these three areas that separate goals or objectives become established. For example, we find some music texts stating that the goals of a kindergarten music program are the developing of beginning music skills, sight-reading and instrumental playing. Such goals are indicative of the approach to teaching which considers the "program" from a logical rather than a psychological point of view. The consequence, however unintended, of such an approach is to place too much emphasis upon the program and too little upon the development or education of the child.

We believe that for the preschool and kindergarten child, music, movement and drama are first and foremost vehicles through which a child is able to express himself, thereby establishing relationships within his environment of people, places and objects. Music, movement and drama are modes of communication as well as of expression and it is important that they be developed as such. The goal, then, becomes one of helping children to express themselves, to communicate, through music, movement and drama.

What do we mean by "expressing themselves"? We mean the communicating of some idea or experience, some inwardly felt emotion, feeling or desire. Young children are spontaneous people and therefore need to be able to express their feelings as they desire, at their time and in their manner. Lest this statement be misinterpreted as being one which advocates complete freedom from control, we want to add that we do not condone those ways of expression which are unnecessarily disturbing to others, still less those that are abusive or destructive. It is the teacher's responsibility to set appropriate standards of conduct in her classroom.

Young children are spontaneous singers especially when they are happy. (This should provide teachers with a clue as to the right kind of classroom atmosphere to generate. Perhaps if there is no singing something could be wrong!) They often sing to themselves as they go about their many and varied activities during each day. The song, or whatever is being "sung," might not always be a recognized tune, if a tune at all, but it has meaning to the singer and the observant, understanding adult appreciates this.

Sylvia Ashton-Warner in *Teacher* wrote of the wonderful spontaneous dancing she used to get from her five-year-old children. It came whenever music was played or sung in her classroom. It was highly individualistic, expressive of the many differing personalities under her care. Drama, of course, may combine both music and movement. Any adult who watches children at play, especially at make-believe play, cannot help but notice in it the elements of drama, music and movement.

If we accept the view that music, movement and drama are interrelated, then how can the teacher foster them as modes of expression in her classroom?

1. First and foremost it is essential that all music, movement and drama be pleasurable experiences for young children. A young child who is unwilling to participate in these kinds of activities should not be forced to do so, nor should he be moved from where the activities are taking place. Rather, he should be allowed to work if he wishes at some other activity of his choice nearby or just to look on. Something of the main activity will "rub-off" on him and eventually he too will participate. It is quite likely that for some time there will not be total class participation in any one activity at any given time. This does not matter provided the non-participating children are interested in what is going on or working at other things.

2. A child's desire to participate in music, drama and movement and the nature of his resulting effort (i.e., its style, performance and direction) is greatly influenced by his societal background. In some areas, for example, and with certain religious groups, dancing is frowned upon by the community. It would be unwise in such cases for a teacher to go against society's wishes. In a similar manner, if music, movement and drama

are not valued in the homes of the majority of children then the ways by which she sets out to develop in her children an interest and a love for them would be much different from the way she would do it if the background of the children were more fortunate.

3. In all activities involving music, movement and drama, the development in the child of creative self-expression is more important than the mechanical imitation of someone else's movements, motions, interpretations. And the educated teacher will certainly not force upon the children patterns to be mechanically imitated. When allowed to be themselves, children's personalities begin to shine; they begin to find out what they can and cannot do; they learn from one another; they begin to try new things. Traditional folk dances, for example the traditional dances of Scotland, and some plays written for young children have little place in the educating of four- and five-year-olds. There is a great variety of "modern" rhythms in the music of television, radio and movies today which lend themselves very well to creative dance. These rhythms are quite infective and are readily accepted by young children.

4. Music, movement and drama assist the child to develop a sense of rhythm. Human actions and activities are at their best when they are rhythmic. Sometimes we call it "timing" as in drama or "beat" or "pulse" as in music. Rhythm permeates all music, movement and drama. When we sing a song, we sing it rhythmically, for if we did not, a great deal of its meaning would be lost. Expressive movement which is intended to communicate is also rhythmic. And so with drama and mime. It all is a matter of timing, of movement in keeping with the plot being communicated. Teachers, therefore, should attempt to highlight the rhythmic aspects of each activity; in singing, they can help the children to feel through all their senses the underlying rhythm of the song; in movement and drama, they can interpret in as dramatically meaningful a way as possible what they are attempting to communicate.

5. Music, movement, and drama all assist in developing the child's senses and his muscular bodily coordination. It is fairly obvious that worthwhile activities in these areas aid in the development of the senses—of hearing (aural discrimination) by recognizing nuances in pitch, tempo, volume, and position,

of seeing (spatial relationships) by developing judgment as to position and of distance, and of large and small muscular coordination through purposefully moving one's body in space. All such development in a positive way has been proven to be essential to future success in other areas of learning. As stated earlier reading experts have shown that the ability to discriminate between sounds, for example, is an essential prerequisite to beginning reading.

6. Encouraging creativity—stretching the young child's imagination to create new, personal ways of expression—is important. It is so easy for a teacher to seek the stereotyped response in music, movement and drama that the imaginative responses frequently are overlooked. There is no one way to enact "Three Billy Goats Gruff" for example, or to sing the little song "The Elephant"[1] which lends itself to wonderful mime.

THE ELEPHANT

Zoë R. Mᶜ Henry

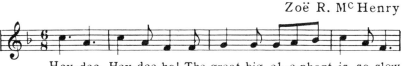

Hey-dee Hey-dee-ho! The great big el- e-phant is so slow

Hey-dee Hey-dee-ho! The el- e-phant is so   slow. He

swings his trunk from side to side as he takes the children for a ride

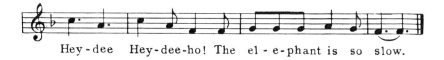

Hey-dee Hey-dee-ho! The el - e-phant is so slow.

[1] Zoë R. McHenry, *Mostly Rhythms* (Melbourne: Whitcombe and Tombs Pty., Ltd.), p. 11. Reprinted by permission of the publisher.

Formal percussion band work in particular tends to be more stereotyped than imaginative and is better left to perfect until after kindergarten. By "formal" here we mean the "school band" of selected players who are trained for special performances. Creative dancing where the child is freely and imaginatively expressing his feelings through movement (which may or may not be done to music) is ideal, both for the developing of imaginative interpretation and for developing a sense of rhythm.

When considering the place of music, movement and drama in communication, teachers should keep the interrelated approach in mind and heed the above six points. If they do so the chances are that subsequent classroom activities will be more effectively directed to the overall goal than if each of the three strands was treated as a separate subject, each with its own, somewhat independent goal. It is necessary, however, at this point to look at each strand separately for there are certain teaching points we would like to make which will result in better teaching, and therefore better learning.

MUSIC

Singing

In preschool and kindergarten singing goes on from time to time all day in a spontaneous way, for young children sing when they are happy, whether it be inside or outside the classroom. It can be said that children use music functionally. There is no one kind of song which is dominant in the early childhood classroom though we feel there should be more emphasis on action and movement songs and singing games rather than on finger plays. Finger plays, though popular with teachers, demand small muscle activities from young children before they really are physically capable of them. This is why action songs and singing games, such as "The Elephant", which call for large muscle movement and give children the opportunity to move and to dramatize, are more suitable.

Singing permeates all aspects of the curriculum. Much of the *planned* singing (those songs, singing games etc., the teacher intends to introduce to the children) should therefore be related to the central theme being developed. Of course there is much singing which is *incidental* to the theme. In this regard it might be appropriate to sing a song about a child's interest as it arises. Teachers need a vast repertoire of songs at their disposal—in fact, memorized—especially for the incidental singing. It is of little value to have to hunt through volumes of song books for a song about something that is interesting to a child at the moment. A well prepared teacher will say "I know a little song about . . . . It goes like this . . . . . ."

Singing should always be pleasurable. It is not necessary for young children to be required to sit still to learn songs in the manner traditional to the authoritarian teacher. It is more often the case than otherwise that only groups of children will be singing at any one time. The others in the class, meanwhile, will be occupied with whatever other tasks interest them.

Songs should not be too long; two verses would usually be the maximum length. Even if they are firm favorites with the teacher long ballads with many verses are not suitable for young children, for singing time is not the time for teachers to perform. It is better to teach a song in its entirety rather than divided into pieces or phrases. It should be repeated frequently during the day rather than practiced over and over again without a break, especially if it is a song that the teacher has planned to be learned because it is about the central theme being developed.

Songs for young children can be about animals, the weather, special festival occasions, the seasons, or can be folk songs, singing games and action songs. The repertoire of the class should vary in rhythm, mood and tempo. Folk songs provide a good source of suitable songs. There are many good anthologies of songs available on the market and each teacher should select from a wide variety of sources. Again it should be stressed that the teacher should not only accumulate but memorize a vast repertoire of songs if she is to be able to utilize singing effectively as a means of communication.

Some hints for the teacher in teaching singing:

1. Make sure those children who want to sing and you are comfortably seated.
2. Sing the song simply but with feeling and rhythm.
3. Do not be worried about the quality of your singing voice, unless, of course, you are unable to carry a tune.
4. Balance quick with slow songs, action songs with quiet ones.
5. Do not be overly concerned with the "growlers" or with children who cannot repeat a tune. Most of them will become better singers in time, given practice and encouragement by a patient and sensitive teacher.

6. Sing songs many times over—young children enjoy the repetition of songs that they like.

Making Music

With young children making music should be the exploring of sounds and rhythms with the voice and selected percussion and melodic instruments.

Children Playing at Rhythm Activities

Indeed the training in aural discrimination which can come from good experiences with sounds and rhythms will have positive value in other areas of learning. Children, though encouraged to spontaneous experimenting with pitch and rhythm instruments, should be led to listen to the dynamics of music: gradations from pp to ff, differences in tonal quality and pitch. They should be able to express these musical elements with their voices and with the percussion and melodic instruments they are acquainted with. Early pitch training is given using question-and-answer kinds of songs such as:

Teacher:

Gen-ev-ieve, Gen-ev-ieve where are you?

Child answers:

Here I am, Here I am, How do you do!

Instruments which can be used with young children include:

1. *Melodic:* tuned bells
xylophones
autoharps
glockenspiels
chime-bars

2. *Percussive:* drums of various sizes
triangles
tambourines
rhythm sticks
jingle bells
coconut shells
wooden blocks
cymbals

Some percussion instruments can be homemade; for example, drums, coconut shells, rhythm sticks (pieces of dowel rods will do well), wooden blocks, shakers (metal bottle tops loosely nailed to a piece of broom handle). Rice or walnut shells in a screw-top jar make a good sound. All instruments used by the children should be available to them at any time during the day. Readers should refer to Emma Sheehy's book *Children Discover Music and Dance* for hints on making drums.[2]

Listening to Music

Young children have been so influenced by television that many of them find it difficult to listen attentively without the visual aspect also being present. Children have to learn to listen just as they have to learn to walk or talk.

Developing the ability to listen and to discriminate differences in sound is the responsibility of the total curriculum. Listening skills are just as important in the playground as they are when "quiet-time" becomes the activity inside the classroom. Teachers have differing points of view on this matter, as witnessed by the classroom practices found today in preschools and kindergartens. Some teachers, for example, allow their children to play a recording at any time during the day. At times this can disturb children who are working at other tasks. Careful supervision is needed to ensure that the activity in this case is purposeful. Other teachers control listening time to such an extent that for a given time the *whole* class is required to listen to the same thing at the same time. Other teachers organize "listening stations" (a record player or tape recorder set up with several earphones for a small group of children to use) in their room, and the listening activity is one of the several group activities the children participate in each day.

Whatever the practice is in the classroom, we feel some listening time related to music is essential, perhaps twice each week. It is during this time that children (in groups or as a class) are encouraged to sit quietly and listen to something until finished. The choice of material to be listened to must be suited to the young child and the activity must be purposeful. There is nothing wrong with the children themselves choosing what they to listen to. Indeed they should be encouraged to do this, for it helps the purposefulness of their listening.

Listening time can be linked with other activities such as movement and art. The children should be asked to listen and then to react (interpret) afterwards. The recording by Winifred Atwell of "Choo Choo Samba," for example, stimulates the children to expres-

---

[2] Emma Sheehy, *Children Discover Music and Dance* (New York: Columbia University Teacher's College, 1971). This is an excellent book for the encouragement of creative music and dance.

sive art work. Similarly Grieg's "Peer Gynt" is good for creative dance. There are many suitable pieces of music with variety in pitch, rhythm and mood, available for listening time activities. They should not be too lengthy for the children.

MOVEMENT

For young children, movement is their bodily responses to music, rhythms, stories, ideas, feelings. Creative dance, with or without musical accompaniment, is one aspect of such movement. It is the bodily exploration of rhythm and space. There are many ways a teacher can help the child respond to rhythms; for example, through songs such as:[3]

THE TIGER

Zoë R. Mc Henry

I'm a great big Ti-ger Creep-ing thru' the jung-le I

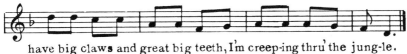

have big claws and great big teeth, I'm creep-ing thru' the jung-le.

With this song the children can enact the words—they can become great big tigers creeping through the jungle. They can vary their movements to suit the sounds, mime the tiger's expressions. There are many similar rhythmic songs suitable for rhythmic dramatization.

Additional methods to help a child respond to rhythms are listed as follows:

1. The rhythmic acting of a story as told by the teacher. Often the teacher may use a percussion instrument, such as a tambourine, to tap out rhythms of the story. The children need plenty of space to move about. Many of their favorite stories,

[3] Zoë R. McHenry, *Kindergarten Hour* (Melbourne Whitcombe and Tombs, Pty, Ltd.), p. 5. Reprinted by permission of the publisher.

e.g., "Peter Rabbit", are most suited to this activity. A piano is not necessary; rather it is better for the teacher to use a small rhythm instrument so as to be able to move around with the children.

2. Movement to music. The aim is to capture the rhythm and mood of the music and to translate it into action. Many favorite old songs and nursery rhymes are suitable. For example: "Hot Cross Buns" and "Twinkle Twinkle Little Star" have a walking rhythm; "The Grand Old Duke of York" has a marching rhythm; "See-Saw, Margery Daw" has a swaying rhythm. The melodies can be played on a piano or other suitable instrument, or a record player. The basic musical notation for the rhythms used is:

FIGURE THIRTEEN

3. Movement associated with rhythmic verse. Select verses with a clear strong rhythm which helps the child to "feel" and respond to it. For example:

SKIPPING

If you can skip on the tip of your toes
I'll give you a ribbon to tie on your bows.
Skip, skip for everyone knows
It's easy to skip on the tip of your toes.

RUNNING

Run, run, run.
Have a little fun
In and out the shadows
In and out the sun.

The teacher would say several of the verses in succession, each with a different rhythm from the one preceding it. For example:

"Hot Cross Buns"	—walk
"Run, run, Run"	—run
"Grand Old Duke of York"	—march
"Skipping"	—skip

A good verse which can be adapted to the four common rhythms is:

Skipping is fun, skipping is fun,
Skipping is fun for everyone.
The longer we skip, the better we skip
So skip, skip, skip.

The word (and subsequently the activity) "skipping" can be varied by substituting "walking", "hopping", "running", etc.

Teaching Hints for Movement

1. The aim of rhythm is to get children to respond differently to differing rhythms. This responding comes gradually and teachers must be patient.
2. Make certain the space to be used is adequate and clearly defined.
3. The children should all move in the same direction so as to avoid collisions.
4. The teacher must say the rhymes in a definite, rhythmic way.
5. The activity should be short and not labored. "Perfection" is a misguiding goal for the teacher of young children. Five minutes for the activity may be more than adequate for this age group.
6. Select some activities that are well suited to out-of-doors.

DRAMA

Young children are forever dramatizing their experiences. At times it is their spontaneous, make-believe way of dealing with a world which they cannot always comprehend or cope with. On the other hand, some of their dramatizing may be the expressive repetition or "recapturing" of what was enjoyed. Another function of drama is that of self and other "exploration," that is, role-playing.

In the classroom spontaneous drama is best seen in the play going on in the play house. The domestic play area is an essential part of every classroom for young children. It is here that children neutralize fears which are paramount in their minds. This is very obvious when one observes, to repeat the example used earlier, how often the three- and four-year-old dramatizes visits to the doctor. Often a child will role-play such a sequence for weeks, never tiring of the repetition. Children, too, will role-play other familiar aspects of their daily lives, and the spontaneous make-believe which develops with other children is essential for the child's total development.

The domestic area should be created in a part of the room where children can feel free of surveillance by teachers and other well-meaning adults. Very often the type of atmosphere which is desirable for imaginative play can be created by the use of cardboard screens or by strategically placed furniture and curtains.

Equipment is necessary in the domestic area but the teacher must strive to achieve a good balance. The imagination of the children should be extended to see possibilities in the use of crude materials and other waste products.

The teacher with her intimate knowledge of her children should aim to introduce different equipment at the *right* time. Children may wish to make things during carpentry work for use in the domestic area, and this type of interest should be fostered.

List of equipment for the domestic area:

Furniture for a playhouse. This can be fashioned with the children from boxes and available properties. Items needed include stove, table, chairs, cupboards, ironing board, beds.

A sink with running water is a great asset but is not always possible. A plastic dish and a jug of water will serve the purpose.

Assortment of dolls, a dolls' bed with linen, dolls' pram and dolls' stroller, doll's bath and clothes. Tray of accessories for doll play— talcum powder tin, cotton, gauze, baby oil bottle, diapers, diaper pins.

A Child Playing in the Housekeeper Corner

Telephone—preferably a real one rather than a toy one.

Large mirror.

Clocks that will wind up.

Laundry set—pegs and clothesline.

First-aid kit—items for a doctors' kit.

Dress-up box: long skirts, vests, dresses, shoes, hats, shirts, neckties, handbags, purses, scarves, ribbons, jewelry, large shopping baskets, plastic string bags.

Not all of the above items will appear simultaneously in the domestic area. The equipment should change as interest varies and the teacher needs to introduce certain objects to stimulate interest. A re-reading of the section dealing with Play in Part One of this book would refresh the reader's thoughts on aspects of spontaneous drama.

Teacher-contrived drama is also important in the classroom. Here the teacher encourages the children to be more original and expansive in their modes of expression. Children enjoy acting known stories but such stories must be those they enjoy and know very well. Because the stories are well known the children are able to become involved in the story and perhaps identify themselves with one or other of the characters. Dressing up helps the child to *become* someone, or something, else. Just the added touch of a hat or cloak, will help the most inhibited child to be more relaxed. "Three Billy Goats Gruff" is a good example of a favorite story which lends itself to dramatic interpretation.

Much of what has been said about movement is applicable also to drama. Children enjoy miming animals and stories about them. The game "What am I"? where children mime an animal, somebody or something they know, will be enjoyed over and over again.

The more mature four- and five-year-old is capable of using puppets most creatively. They can make their own puppets from papier-mache using, say, the cylinder from toilet rolls as a base. Certainly the puppets will be elementary models of what they are supposed to represent, but this does not matter. The objective of puppet drama is to give the children another avenue through which to express their experiences. The quality of the puppet is therefore of secondary importance. It is better for the children to make their own puppets than to use those commercially produced, for in the process of making them the puppet becomes "alive" to the child. Painting the features on the puppet and dressing it make it all the more personal; the puppet gains all the more character when the child undertakes its creation.

Hints for the Teacher

1. Build up a repertoire of simple stories known and enjoyed by young children. Such stories become the basis for subsequent drama, mime, puppetry.

2. Gather a "property box" of old clothing—hats, shawls, handbags, shoes, ties, beads and old jewelery, for use by the children. Have the "property box" readily accessible to the children. Clean it out periodically and keep adding new "properties."

3. Cardboard cartons and large building blocks are good for representing buildings, caves, etc.

4. For use in the playground, an old car body (painted with lead-free paint) with the doors removed is valuable. Objects such as a model airplane, constructed by a talented parent, are ideal for the spontaneous dramatic play which children enjoy so much.

SUMMARY

We said earlier that music, movement and drama are modes not only of expression but also of communication where the child is communicating his thoughts, feelings, and desires to others. The teacher's responsibility is to help the child develop his confidence and skills in expressing himself and to make his communication with others more unique, more expressive, more natural. To do this there must be constant experiencing by the child of music, movement and drama. For how can we know what we can do if we are never given the opportunities and encouragement to try?

BIBLIOGRAPHY

Aronoff, Frances Webber. *Music and Young Children*. New York: Holt, Rinehart, & Winston, 1969.

Chandler, Bessie E. *Early Learning Experiences*. Dansville, New York: The Instructor Publications, Inc., 1970, pp. 9-35.

Gell, Heather. *Music, Movement and the Young Child*, rev. ed. Sydney: Australasian Publishing Company, 1959.

Leeper, Sarah H.; Dales, Ruth; Skipper, Dora; Witherspoon, Ralph. *Good Schools for Young Children*. New York: The Macmillan Co., 1968.

Molony, Eileen, editor. *How to Form a Playgroup*. London: British Broadcasting Commission, 1970, Chapter 5.

Rogers, Vincent R. *Teaching in the British Primary School*. London: The Macmillan Co., 1970, Chapter 11.

Sheehy, Emma. *Children Discover Music and Dance*. New York: Columbia University Teachers College, 1968.

Taylor, Barbara J. *A Child Goes Forth*. Provo, Utah: Brigham Young University Press, 1970, Chapter 4.

CHAPTER THREE

The Development of Communication through Art

When considering how young children attempt to communicate through art, one needs to look again at the whole development of the child. Art educators generally agree that there are broad developmental stages in children's art ranging from a purely manipulative stage to one of pictorial composition. The stages characteristic of children of nursery school and kindergarten age are the manipulative and the symbolic. Gaitskell and Hurwitz have divided the manipulative stage into three phases through which the child progresses: from random manipulation to controlled manipulation and finally to named manipulation.[1] We will here, however, consider the manipulative stage as a whole and then the symbolic stage.

THE MANIPULATIVE STAGE

This is the stage where young children touch, bang, mold, squeeze. It is a most important stage for here is laid the very basis for meaningful expression in the child's later development. It is the *process* that is important in these early manipulative experiences. It matters not whether the child is working with "gluggy" finger paint, or "squelchy" clay; he will not be overly concerned with his end product—this concern will come later in his development. He is, however, concerned with manipulating the material, finding out what it is, how it "works" and what he can do with it. He builds up a knowledge through experimentation. Much incidental learning takes place as the child is manipulating media. For example he becomes conscious of colors, of texture and other attributes of the media. At the same

---

[1] Charles D. Gaitskell and Al Hurwitz, *Children and Their Art,* 2d ed. (New York: Harcourt, Brace, Jovanovich, 1970), pp. 142-46.

time he unconsciously develops preferences for certain media and seeks these out.

The muscular coordination which develops as a result of these manipulative experiences will be utilized fully in successive stages of his growth and development.

THE SYMBOLIC STAGE

It is thrilling to watch young children as they begin symbolic art work. They will set out confidently to paint some particular thing and be very satisfied with their efforts. Usually there is a complete lack of frustration on the part of the child who indeed feels himself to be in command of the situation. There is no set or fixed age when the symbolic stage emerges. Indeed a four-year-old can say "I am going to draw a witch!" and may confidently draw something quite unintelligible to others yet which for him quite satisfactorily represents or symbolizes a witch.

Once young children realize that they can create whatever they desire, they will often spend longer periods at an activity and do several drawings of the same topic. It is at this stage that children will ask the teacher to write a name or short story underneath their work.

AN ART ENVIRONMENT

It is vital that teachers create a secure environment which offers art activities suited to the developmental level and needs of young children. Most teachers have at some time come into contact with a young child who is reluctant to enter into art activities. This can occur if the child has come from a home environment where standards beyond his actual development and skills have been prematurely inflicted or where "messy play," such as mud pies and water play, have been frowned upon. To children media such as finger paints and clay can be repugnant, and the teacher should avoid forcing or coercing a child into participating in the activity. The provision of waterproof overalls has a freeing effect and develops a sense of security especially for children who fear a reprimand over soiled clothes. Overcoming such a fear takes time but a relaxed, secure environment will help diminish inhibitions.

There are other factors which adversely influence the child. One of these is the widespread use of coloring books. Often the child has been given these books at too early an age, by well meaning parents. The child tries to reproduce the adult forms represented in the coloring books and in doing so inhibits his own expression. Instead of delightfully spontaneous representations one observes stereotyped "copied" ones. Coloring books and other adult patterning, including work books, should never be expected from young children in any area of learning under any circumstance. Parents as well as teachers should be educated in this regard. Discussions on child art should be included in parent-teaching meetings; and the damaging effects of coloring books, adult patterning and similar activities be fully explained to parents.

Another cause of attitudes which inhibit art can arise if adults, unwittingly or wittingly criticize or laugh at a child's art efforts. Peer pressure or criticism from siblings also can have an inhibiting effect. Often, too, in a situation where children are allowed to follow their own interest and select a preferred activity, it is not unusual to find children ignoring the art area and instead turning, perhaps for a while exclusively, to some other kind of material, such as blocks or domestic toys. These children will after a period usually play-out their preference and turn to art. It is usually the immature child who is more inclined to keep to the one activity (usually with manipulative material) whereas the more mature child will sample many, trying them out. The observant teacher may learn something valuable from this simple fact.

Above all children should feel free from pressure and free from interference. They should not be asked to hurry to complete their work in order to embark on another activity; the timetable must be flexible so that children can be allowed time to finish the work on hand. The teacher needs to be sensitive to the special needs of each moment. She must sense when she is needed and when not to intrude. The child who is intent on a painting should not be distracted by questions. If he wants to share his feelings while he is working on his picture—or after he has completed it—this will become obvious from his actions.

The teacher should avoid offering technical advice on such matters as filling up the paper or lining in the sky. Advice on matters of technique has no place in art work with young children. Indeed it is likely to affect their development adversely.

Given the right environment and offered the right experiences the creative expression of young children will flourish. Much will depend on the sensitivity and awareness of the teacher who by creating an environment where children feel free to explore and experiment will foster creative growth through art.

SETTING THE SCENE FOR ART WORK WITH YOUNG CHILDREN

Young children are spontaneous, active and often boisterous. They will usually engage in activities with great zest and enthusiasm. They will bubble over with delight as they experience a new art activity for the first time and will want to share their discovery with a friend or the teacher. When planning the physical layout of the room the teacher must consider the nature of young children and plan accordingly.

Establishing an Art Area in the Classroom

In order to develop art experiences in a classroom for young children, it is necessary to consider first the general organization of the room, and second what experiences other than art are being planned.

During free activity periods there should be opportunity for the children to participate in art activities. (Part Three of this book elaborates on organization and management.) It is essential that there should be some clearly defined area where art activities are done. This area should be located away from the busyness of the block play areas. Above all, it should be out of the way of traffic moving to and from doors. Children need ample space for art, and the teacher should concern herself to provide it.

There needs to be space in the art area for the displaying of children's work. Some young children like to take their work home but others will enjoy seeing it displayed for a short period and proudly bring mother into the classroom to see it.

Providing the Right Materials and Equipment

Young children should be encouraged to help in the organization of art activities and in cleaning up after them. For this reason materials should be stored in cupboards on shelves which are within the reach of the children.

Wherever possible children should be encouraged to participate in the making of certain materials. For example, the recipe for dough

A Display of Children's Art Work

and finger paint should be displayed and referred to as the teacher and children mix the ingredients together. The making of finger paint, dough and paste should be done in a special place and an area of the wall used for displaying recipes.

Arrangements need to be made for the drying of wet work. A hanging clothes line with clothes pins on it is useful for this purpose. Aprons are essential materials for painting and for other messy activities. As we have said before the child needs to feel secure from worry about soiling clothes. The practice of using cloth aprons or large shirts is not always practical, for paint can seep through them. A thick plastic or oil baize smock made as shown is more successful.

The following is a list of basic materials for beginning art work with young children.

Easels: These should be constructed of metal or wood, be approximately six inches higher than the child's head and be at least two feet wide. The paint containers should not be on a ledge in the front of the easel, but should be in containers placed on a table

FIGURE FOURTEEN

at the right hand side of the easel (the left-hand side for left-handed children).

Brushes: These should be round handled, 10 to 12 inches long and ½ to 1 inch in brush width. Finer brushes should be included when the child has developed a degree of manipulative skill.

Paint: Both liquid and powder paint are necessary. Primary colors should be introduced first, and the children encouraged when they are ready to experiment and to mix the secondary colors for themselves.

Paint containers: Milk cartons cut off and joined together with heavy duty tape form a good base for babyfood jars or other small jars in which the paint is placed. Small quantities of paint, approximately one inch in depth, should be placed in the containers as children cannot safely handle deep quantities of paint. Messy brushes and messy hands can have a distracting effect on the child. An aluminum cupcake set is ideal for dry paint technique where colors are mixed by the child as he works.

Paper: White paper makes the best background for children's drawing and finger painting. Awareness of color and sensitiveness to it is an integral part of art experiences. It is aided best by the use of white paper. However, colored construction paper and brown paper may be needed for collage work. The size of paper is an important consideration when working with young children. As a general rule the younger the child the larger should be the paper. A good beginning is to have paper over 2 feet in length. The shape of the paper is important; it should be rectangular. A square shape should be avoided as it is difficult to use compositionally and is unlike the books and writing pages which the child will later use. Teachers should vary the way they pin the paper to the easel placing it sometimes horizontally and sometimes vertically. For larger work, such as murals, large pieces of paper can be spread on the floor or on low tables.

Other Materials Needed for the Art Area:

    Paste
    Glue
    Large lumber crayons
    Chalk
    Earth clay
    Flour
    Salt

Children Engaging in a Group Activity Using Scrap Materials

WASTE MATERIALS AND COLLAGE WORK

An art medium often overlooked by many teachers is the collage. It is necessary to provide waste material of all kinds for collage work. These materials can be collected from the children's homes and from other sources in the community. The materials should be arranged according to type and size and then stored in containers accessible to the children. Classifying the material can be done according to type; for example: nature materials, fabrics, styrofoam, scraps of colored paper, and so on. The teacher should strive to make the children aware of texture, size, weight and other properties of the objects by direct observation and discussion as things are added to the collections. Edible things, such as rice, beans and popcorn should not be used as children are tempted to eat them.

The following is a list of material suitable for use in collage work:

Newspapers

Colored paper from magazines

Margarine cartons

Plastic ice cream containers

Styrofoam containers

Pieces of scrap fabric

Cardboard boxes

Pieces of corrugated cardboard

Cardboard roll from the center of the toilet rolls and paper towels

Old buttons

Empty cotton spools

Colored paper, e.g. candy wrappers

Pieces of ribbon

Scrap pieces of wallpaper

Pine cones

Egg shells

Tooth picks

Shells

Leaves

Pieces of bark

Stones

Sticks

Sand

Flowers

Feathers

Moss

Ferns

Pipe cleaners

Pieces of soft wire

Old tooth brushes

Paper plates

Napkins

WHAT ART EXPERIENCES SHOULD
WE OFFER TO YOUNG CHILDREN?

There are four main art experiences well suited to the developmental needs of young children. If used constantly these four activities will stimulate creativeness within the child and foster his growth through art.

1. Drawing
2. Painting: (A) easel, with brushes, (B) with fingers
3. Modelling
4. Collage work

Many teachers of young children strive to think of constantly new art ideas to offer to young children. Too zealous a search for novelty can easily result in being merely "gimmicky." Rather than fostering art development, too many art forms introduced over too short a period can have the opposite effect, even to retarding growth. Only through constant use of an art medium can the child gain mastery of it. Once this mastery has been gained the child becomes more self-confident and more resourceful, and therefore more creative. He is ready to move on to more skillfully controlled and more expressive activities using the materials and techniques over which he has developed some mastery. Although the four mentioned art activities are constantly offered to all children, they need not be the same for each child. The teacher must be ever watchful to see when a new stage of readiness has emerged and be able to provide for new demands as they arise.

Let us now look more closely at the four main art activities for young children.

Drawing

Large stubby crayons and large sheets of white paper should be available to the child from the time he first is able to grasp a writing instrument and can make marks on paper. For the young nursery school child this activity is best done standing at an easel. Large pieces of paper can also be pinned on "building board" or other soft lining board, if easel space is scarce. The standing position is better because it facilitates large muscle movements. Most five-year-old children in kindergarten have muscle control established well enough to be able to draw with lumber crayons at small tables.

GENERAL POINTS

1. The teacher should not offer technical advice to the child.
2. The paper used should be rectangular in shape for two reasons: it makes composition easier, and the shape is that which the children will encounter in reading and writing.
3. The teacher should not question the child about his drawing. If he wants to talk about his work the teacher should be receptive and interested.

Painting with Brushes

This is one of the very best kinds of art experiences for young children as the fluid medium of paint suits the temperament and mode of creative expression of the young. In the manipulative stage the child finds intense satisfaction just from the application of colors.

GENERAL POINTS

1. Painting at an easel should be introduced with one or two colors and the range of colors built up over a period as the children gain skill in handling the medium.
2. Each new color should be discussed as it is introduced.

Children Painting at Easels

3. After painting routines have been established the children should participate in the mixing of colors.

4. Children should reach a point where they select and mix colors which they like and which are expressive of mood and situation.

5. Children should always wash their brushes and assist in the general clean up.

6. Overall smocks should be worn by the children during painting activities.

7. Easels should be placed in a position where they obtain good lighting.

Painting With Fingers

This is an excellent art experience which gives young children valuable kinesthetic experiences. Finger painting can be done on paper or directly onto tables. However, to gain maximum benefit the surface should be white so that the true brilliance of the colors will be seen. A sheet of thick white plastic placed over the table will serve this purpose.

Children Painting Blocks of Various Shapes

GENERAL POINTS

1. Children should stand at tables to obtain free muscular movement of the arms and back.

2. Children should use both hands.

3. Two colors should be used with a spoonful of each colored finger paint placed apart on the surface. Children may then observe the changing colors as they blend together.

4. Children should not sprinkle dry powdered paint onto an uncolored finger paint base. First, powdered paint while being sprinkled can be inhaled by the children. (Even if nontoxic paint is used it is still highly undesirable for it to be inhaled.) Second, one of the chief values of finger painting is the emotional satisfaction not only from the creation of the "painting" but even more perhaps from the delightful tactual-motor experience of applying the paint. The sprinkling of paint and the use of shakers can detract from this experience.

5. Children should have wet hands to begin finger painting. The finger paint will then feel less slimy.

6. Buckets of water should be placed close by so that children

can use it to wet their hands before beginning painting, to soften the finger paint if necessary, and finally for cleaning up the tables.

7. To allow children a sense of freedom and security a plastic overall is necessary. Sleeves should be rolled up before the children begin painting.

OTHER ART EXPERIENCES USING FINGER PAINTS

Finger paint printing. This is a technique using finger paint. The method is as follows:

1. Make a finger painting on a table.
2. Place a piece of white paper over the finger paint.
3. Place a piece of cardboard of the same size over the paper and press very firmly all over.
4. Remove the cardboard and lift up the piece of paper. The print should be clear.
5. Allow to dry.

Hand prints. Children enjoy seeing their hand prints. This can be done on pieces of paper, with the children's names printed underneath. It can also be done on fabric. If curtains for windows or cupboards are printed in this way, each child will be able to see his hand and name in print.

Covering boxes. Cardboard cartons for waste material collections as well as dress-up and other boxes can be covered with finger paint prints cut to size. Each box can then be labelled.

Recipes for finger paint.

1. *Cornstarch finger paint*

   Mix ½ cup cornstarch with enough cold water to make a paste; add 3 cups of boiling water. Allow mixture to boil briefly. Tempera paint or on occasion food dyes may be added for color. Children enjoy seeing the dramatic color change with food dyes. A small amount of antiseptic will help the mixture keep longer.

2. *Liquid starch finger paint*

   Pour required amount of commercial liquid starch into a container and add color. Pour mixture directly on to a wet surface.

3. *Wallpaper paste finger paint*

Prepare as for wallpaper paste only make the solution thinner by adding more water. Mix until lumps disappear and add required color.

Modelling Experiences

EARTH CLAY

All young children should experience the sensation of working with clay. The pounding, squeezing and molding provide excellent muscular movement as well as a great outlet for frustrations. Clay requires careful storage and is best kept in an earthenware jar with a tight fitting lid. If a jar is not available an aluminum garbage can with a lid makes a good substitute. After being used clay is best kept in round balls with a thumb indentation in each filled with water. A piece of thick moistened fabric should be placed over the top of the clay. If a piece of polythene plastic is spread over the fabric the clay should store well.

GENERAL POINTS

1. When beginning working with clay children should get into the habit of wedging; that is, pounding it on the table, to free it from air bubbles.
2. For most young children the first exploration with clay will be purely manipulative.
3. Do not give the children modelling tools. Clay should be worked with the hands only.
4. As with all art media for young children it is the *process* not the product which is of paramount importance.
5. Earth clay stimulates creative activity far more than does dough or plasticine. Earth clay should always be available to children.
6. Children should learn that earth clay requires special storing. Ultimately they should be capable of looking after it themselves.

MODELLING WITH SALT-FLOUR DOUGH

Young children enjoy modelling with this medium. Where possible it should be associated with the housekeeping area. Cookie cutters, mixing bowls and other cooking utensils should be available to the children when they use dough. It should be remembered that dough is not a substitute for clay.

Recipe for Salt-Flour dough

2 cups flour
1 cup salt
Small amount antiseptic
Food dye or powder paint
Enough water to make a firm dough.
Keep extra flour at hand as the mixture can become sticky.

Collage Work

Collage work can be introduced successfully with very young children, and early activities can include the tearing of colored paper and pasting onto large sheets of paper. In their first attempts, most children will paste on the scraps at random and will need some guidance on the use of paste. The act of tearing the paper is in itself particularly good for developing manipulative skill.

After the children gain confidence in working with torn paper, pieces of fabric cut in irregular shapes and sizes by the teacher can be added. The fabric used should vary in texture and children should be encouraged to talk about the differences in texture. Other materials should be added as the teacher gauges the children's readiness for them. Eventually a wide selection of materials should be provided.

GENERAL POINTS

1. When the children have sufficient manipulative skill they should be given good quality, round nosed scissors that cut well.

2. The child must make his own discoveries. The teacher should not dictate the patterns or make prescriptive suggestions to him.

3. It will be necessary to provide other working tools at the collage table: staplers, scotch-tape, paste brushes, glue, slide-on paper clips.

4. The teacher should always be available to help if assistance is needed when gluing material together.

5. Edible articles such as popcorn, beans, dried cereals, etc., should *not* be used.

CREATIVE PUPPET WORK

This kind of art experience will grow out of the work of the collage area. As with other media children should make their own discoveries as to what they can do with the materials supplied and the encouragement given by the teacher. The introduction of paper bags into the collage area is often a good way of stimulating puppet making. A face is painted on the paper bag, which is then placed over the hand.

GROUP EXPERIENCES IN ART

Group experiences should be encouraged and with kindergarten age children there is a great deal of scope for this. Group art experiences should begin with two or three children. An exciting happening, a special visitor or an incident from a favorite story are good topics for murals undertaken as a group project.

GENERAL POINTS

1. Paint and collage are good media for introducing group art experiences.
2. Children need to plan their "picture" and to allot areas of work before beginning the job.
3. Results of these group activities should be shared with the rest of the class.

SUMMARY

We have tried to point out several important features of art communication for the young child. In summary these are:

1. Children's art is most developmental.
2. Children need to experience and experiment with art constantly in order that they might communicate through it.
3. For children to grow through art there needs to be an environment which fosters it.
4. The role of the teacher in art is crucial. The right kinds of opportunities for experiencing art must be given the child to

ensure positive growth through art. Much damage to a child's expressive communication can be done by poor teaching.

5. As art is a mode of communication there is a definite link with language development—first through oral language and later through written language.

BIBLIOGRAPHY

Association for Childhood Education International. *Creating with Materials for Work and Play.* Bulletin Number 5. Washington, D.C.: Association for Childhood Education International, 1957.

Chandler, Bessie. *Early Learning Experiences.* Dansville, New York: The Instructor Publications, Inc., 1970.

Derham, Frances. *Art for the Child under Seven.* Canberra: Australian Preschool Association, 1967.

Dimmack, Max. *Modern Art Education in the Primary School.* Melbourne: The Macmillan Co., 1958.

Gaitskell, Charles D., and Hurwitz, A. L. *Children and Their Art,* 2d ed. New York: Harcourt, Brace, Jovanovich, 1970.

Hoover, Frances L. *Art Activities for the Very Young.* Worcester, Massachusetts: Davis Publishing Co., 1961.

Leeper, Sarah H.; Dales, Ruth; Skipper, Dora; and Witherspoon, Ralph. *Good Schools for Young Children.* New York: The Macmillan Co., 1968.

Lowenfeld, Victor, and Brittain, W. Lambert. *Creative and Mental Growth,* 5th ed. New York: The Macmillan Co., 1970

McFee, June King. *Preparation for Art.* San Francisco: Wadsworth Publishing Co., 1961.

Plaskow, Daphne. *Children and Creative Activity.* London: The Society for the Education through Art, 1970.

SECTION B

The Development of an Awareness and Understanding of the Environment

CHAPTER FOUR

Introduction

As we have said earlier in this part, young children need to learn to understand their environment. We have said also that to the very young child the environment is an undifferentiated whole. Adults know, and the growing child more and more comes to realize, that there is so much to discover, to learn about, to become interested in, to explore and to experiment with.

For a long time teachers have selected aspects of the environment as they, educated adults, experience it to be, and have given more or less effective consideration to ways of helping children to a greater knowledge and understanding of their own, that is, each child's, environment. But the child's environment is what it is for the child. It will differ from child to child, and differ even more from the environment the teacher knows and understands.

This is a difficult yet profoundly important principle. Failure to appreciate its significance and to teach in the light of it is responsible for the lack of realism, for children, in so much of the logically sequential (to adults) topics of a curriculum. In science, for example, the dreariness of memorizing words may be science for the teacher but is for some children little more than words to give back on demand.

As we said earlier, the environment to the very young child is a largely undifferentiated whole. As he grows in experience and in abilities, his environment, that is, the whole world as the child knows it, becomes far richer and more complex. But at the age of four or five his environment is still largely a "whole" and learning about it is best grasped by the child if the teacher uses an integrated approach. For example, the teacher's introduction into the classroom of the study of ants, if it captures the children's imaginations, could lead to the development of a variety of learning situations. Something might have been said or asked by the children about ants, and the interest might be such that the teacher brings a colony of ants, suitably housed for observation, into the classroom. If the teacher lacked imagination and thought only of *science* and thirty minute *lessons,* she might succeed in "imparting" quite a number of facts about ants. She also runs no small risk of so surfeiting the children that their appetite for learning about ants is dulled more or less permanently.

The teacher of young children will think of and treat ants not as one "topic" in a "subject." Ants will be, if the children's interest is a lively one, a "center of interest" around which the teacher can lead the children into a variety of activities which adults call language, number, art, science, social studies, and so on.

Teaching this way is not easy. In fact the demands made upon the teacher—demands upon her time in preparation, her ingenuity in planning new avenues for exploration, and especially upon her knowledge about the environment—far exceed what is expected of her in the unimaginative teaching mentioned earlier. The teacher needs to be *sensitive to the environment* not only as an educated adult but also as one aware of its potentialities for satisfying and developing the interests of young children. She needs, and this is crucial, to have understanding and knowledge of what three-, four-, five-, and six-year-old children like to see, hear, and do as well as what they are able to understand if she is to be an effective teacher in an open-ended teaching situation.

Let us look at how the environment can be used to further the children's knowledge of mathematics, of science and of social living. There may be some repetition of statements for this cannot be avoided. Where it has been avoided the reader is asked to see for himself the possible integration of ideas.

BIBLIOGRAPHY

Gans, Roma; Stendler, Celia; Almy, Millie. *Teaching Young Children.* Yonkers-on-Hudson, New York: World Book Co., 1952.

Leeper, Sarah; Dales, Ruth; Skipper, Dora; and Witherspoon, Ralph. *Good Schools for Young Children.* New York: The Macmillan Co., 1968.

Rogers, Vincent R. "The New Mathematics." In *Teaching in the British Primary School.* London: The Macmillan Co., 1970.

The Schools Council. *Mathematics in the Primary Schools.* Curriculum Bulletin Number 1. London: Her Majesty's Stationery Office, 1969.

Tarnay, Elizabeth D. *What Does the Nursery School Teacher Teach?* New York: National Association for the Education of Young Children, 1965, Number 106.

CHAPTER FIVE

The Development of an Understanding of Mathematics in the Child's Environment[1]

PLANNING THE CURRICULUM

We are aware of the existence of some good quality commercially produced programmed work in mathematics for the young child in kindergarten. We do not intend to deal fully with this kind of mathematical programming here for the purpose and scope of such programs are clearly outlined in each of the currently available textual series in mathematical learning. We would like to say that, wisely used, such programmed work can be excellent aids to learning. It should be understood, however, that they are, because of their nature, contrived programs which take little account of whatever is distinctive about the children in a classroom group—indeed they cannot and should not be expected to. It is the job of the teacher, not of the program, to know and care for the special abilities and defects, and the particular interests of her children. The good teacher is far more than an assembly line worker, following the lockstep of someone else's program. But the lockstep is inevitable if commercially produced programs are followed slavishly without sufficient thought as to the age and aptitude of the children being taught. Such programs are followed slavishly, also, because many teachers do not understand clearly enough the *ideas* (concepts) that the program, or apparatus, or drill are supposed to help children to grasp. But again, we want to stress that used wisely such programs of work can be of great help to the teacher and the child. They are certainly not being used wisely if, quite unmodified, they are the sole source of topics, methods and practice in any classroom.

---

[1] Some of the material for this chapter has been adapted and reprinted from Frederick N. Ebbeck "Mathematics in the Primary Grades," *The Instructor* (January 1974). Reprinted by permission of Instructor Publications, Inc., Dansville, New York.

How can they be used wisely in the kindergarten? To begin with they must be adapted to suit the needs of the individual child and be used in accordance with what the teacher knows of the child's previous experience and level of attainment. In mathematics more than in any other area it is vital that teachers have a systematic program in operation in their classroom, but this does not mean that all children are working systematically through any one text at the same time. This is not only foolish, it is impossible to ensure. Rather, it is necessary that the teacher first knows what concepts, processes and facts young children need to acquire in order for them to progress to higher levels of learning. Second, the teacher must *know how to plan learning experiences for the development* of these concepts, and third, she must learn how to find out, *for each child,* whether he understands the ideas and processes the teacher wants him to understand and can employ, with understanding, the skills he has been practicing. Good planning might well use a children's textbook as the basis of the development of the concept, process or fact. Then again the teacher might use a textbook as supplementary, or not at all. Further, she might decide against using someone else's program. What is central to the whole problem of planning a systematic program in mathematics, or any area of learning for that matter, is that the work must be well thought out in advance, be sequential in development and be adapted by the teacher to the needs of the individual child.

In summary form, the mathematical concepts, processes and facts which we want our young children to know by the time they are about six or seven years old are:

1. Sorting and classifying objects into sets. Comparing sizes of two sets (the number of objects in each set) by matching or one-to-one correspondence; learning the language, and later the symbols, of inequality; is greater than $>$, is less than $<$.

2. Counting the number of objects in a set (cardinal numbers). This, in effect, involves putting each object into one-to-one correspondence with one in the series of number names. Conservation of number. Composition of numbers up to 20 known without counting on or counting back.

3. The number line, numbers in sequence or in order up to 100 (ordinal numbers). "Nodding acquaintance" with numbers beyond 20 but, except for a few children, no written manipulation of these numbers in isolation from experience. Growing awareness of place-value in the number notation.

4. Measurement and money. Conservation of measures. Knowledge of the relationships between one unit and another (the common units of weights and measures which normally come within the experience of young children).

5. Simple fractions: halves, quarters, three-quarters.

6. Varied aspects of the operations of addition, subtraction, multiplication and division as these arise in the real situations of the classroom.

7. Shape and size (proportion).[2]

A knowledge and understanding of the basic concepts, processes and facts which the teacher hopes to teach her children *over a period of time* enables her to plan for their development. We have already said that one aspect of such planning involves the construction of a mathematical curriculum which *may or may not* follow any one textbook.

A second, very important aspect, especially where young children are concerned, is the mathematics which evolves *incidentally* throughout each school day. "Incidentally" here means as it happens to come about, as the moment arises, as the situation develops. It may or may not fit in with a program such as that set out above. Yet it is the kind of learning which has been taking place in the child's home before he begins schooling though, perhaps, the correct mathematical terminology has been absent.

Incidental learning, especially for the young, is indispensable to the development of mathematical insight. Indeed, Piaget has made clear to us that the pre-operational and intuitive-operational phases in a child's development (usually from ages 3+ to 5+) are those during which intuitive thinking begins to emerge. If this is so, then incidental learning of mathematics, where the mathematical experience presented to the child has a meaningful (environmental) context as well as being represented in a concrete manner with a minimum of perceptual difficulties, leads the child imperceptibly, without strain and bewilderment, towards the clearer, more powerful abstractions which are the essence of mathematical knowledge.

Incidental learning (or for the teacher, the capitalizing on the incidental), should permeate all the activities of the classroom. Such learning should not be relegated to fixed times in a classroom timetable. It provides opportunities for a meaningful and interesting in-

---

[2] The Schools Council, Publication, *Mathematics in Primary Schools.* Curriculum Bulletin Number 1 (London: Her Majesty's Stationery Office, 1969), pp. 11-12. Reprinted by permission of the Controller of Her Majesty's Stationery Office.

troduction to topics which ultimately have to find their place in the logical system of ideas which a well planned, sequential mathematics program hopes to develop for each child. The good teacher who capitalizes on the incidental learning in mathematics sees the significance of learning in a meaningful context and is better able to develop such a well planned, sequential program. She does this because she knows her children well, she knows what mathematics is all about and is able to see mathematical significance in incidents when it arises. Incidental learning of mathematics is not something which is haphazard, although it can become haphazard if it is kept at the surface level where the insights of the children are not developed to a greater depth.

The nature and value of incidental learning in mathematics may be more clearly seen from an example. The following incidents of everyday school life are taken from the diary of a teacher. They illustrate the use teachers can make of centers of interest and of children's curiosity and desire to explore; the important part two way communication plays in mathematical learning; the talk that goes on between child and child, teacher and child. They show how everyday happenings in a classroom can be harnessed to mathematical ends.

1. Helen and Chris wanted to do some measuring with the trundle wheel. They said they wanted to find out how long and how wide the grass plot outside the classroom was. But the trundle wheel was being used by someone else. "Never mind," said Helen, "we'll use the yard stick. It's just the same." The group that had commandeered the trundle wheel were out measuring the playground and found it to be forty yards long and forty yards wide. I suggested Helen and Chris find the perimeter by using the trundle wheel. John, from the other group, said, "No need. It's a square so it must be forty times four. That is 160 yards."

2. Here the children were experimenting with water. They found that a small watering can had to be filled twice to fill a pint container. And they found a cup had to be filled twice to fill a pint container. It dawned on them that the watering can and the cup each held half a pint. They proved it by filling the watering can sixteen times to fill a gallon container. Later they filled a tiny baby food jar nineteen times to fill the pint container. I asked how much water it held. The children found this question difficult. I said, "If you fill the

one-quarter pint container four times to fill the pint container we say it holds a quarter pint. If you fill the watering can twice to fill the pint container, we say it holds a half pint." Immediately Kenneth said, "I know, the little jar holds one nineteenth of a pint."

3. It was Martin's birthday and he brought a large bag of candy to be shared. He was five years old. I asked him to weigh the sweets and he found them to weigh one pound. He said, "Shall I count them?" I agreed, though I knew he'd probably get muddled in the process. Seven children were now around us, so I explained how much quicker and easier counting was when we count in tens. The children made up groups of tens. Martin said, "I've got some here that don't make ten." Here was my opportunity to talk about tens and units. We went on to make sixty-four and showed this number on the abacus. The children seemed to understand.

4. Sometimes the children are directed to choose any mathematical tool (e.g. trundle wheel, thermometer) and work with it. Robert chose the letter balance. When he brought it into the classroom Kevin said, "I've seen one of those in the Post Office." I naturally asked what it was used for. He said, "For weighing letters." I asked why it couldn't be used for weighing parcels and immediately Keith said, "It only weighs up to nine ounces." Robert was quite a long while before he decided what to weigh. He was obviously looking for something light. He weighed his number book—it was one-half ounce—and then he weighed a plastic cup—it was seven-eighths of an ounce. He was stumped with this calculation. I explained to him about eighths—the eight divisions of an ounce—and demonstrated with a piece of paper folded into eight. I wanted to find out if he understood so I asked him to find how much heavier the cup was than his book. He soon returned with the answer—three-eighths of an ounce.

As we have said, programming for mathematics in any grade, for any age, cannot be haphazard. Capitalizing on incidental happenings in an early childhood classroom demands careful thinking on the teacher's part. It also demands preparation of a meaningful learning environment. As centers of interest begin, such as those indicated in the foregoing examples—measuring length and capacity using objects, Martin's birthday, an interest in some tool or device—the teacher must be prepared in her mind to see mathematical significance within these interests. For example, if an interest centers on "the seaside," "people who help us," and countless other topics, the teacher must be one jump ahead of the children, as it were, and be able to plan and subtly direct the course the interest takes so that some real mathematical learning happens. She cannot wait with arms folded expecting a miracle. Rather, her role is to see that things *do* happen.

PROVISION OF MATERIALS

As well as a thorough understanding of the concepts, processes and facts that she wants each child to develop during this preschool and kindergarten period, she needs to plan for the teaching of these in a variety of situations. Such planning would include the *provision of materials*. Curious, active, talkative, inquiring children must be surrounded by things that evoke questions; by materials that invite manipulation; by situations that call for exploration. It is a teacher's job to provide these.

Sand, water, clay, wood are materials which should be available to the child every day. Each material has special properties of its own and the young child needs to handle it and explore it to find out for himself what he can do with it. Very often this early exploratory stage seems a messy one to adult eyes, and teachers sometimes underestimate its value.

Other material, including living things such as animals that live in the woods, in walls, under stones, children's pets, and seeds, bulbs, plants, sprouting acorns, and many more should be used to develop the child's ideas of number, weight, size, volumes, and, if living, rates of growth and speeds of movement. All these help the child's mathematical development and give opportunities for further meaningful growth.

An important responsibility for the teacher is the provision of appropriate mathematical tools. These should be of good quality. Schools could have a central store for the most expensive ones, to be borrowed when required, but the everyday ones should be in each classroom.

When mathematical tools are to be used in the classroom, the teacher should explain, always with what help the children are able to give, the function and construction of each tool. This explanation should not be highly technical nor done for all children at the same time. Some tools to be provided include:

a trundle wheel   "leggo" blocks
map measures   oven for cooking
balances of several kinds   surveyor's tape
candy thermometer   globes
timers   atlases
three-dimensional figures   hour glasses
  (some solid and others   stop watches
    hollow plastic   levers
    capable of being filled)   magnets
compasses   money
pulleys   bathroom scales
clock faces   building blocks
shapes (solid)   tape measures
counters of many kinds   "seriation" block sets
calenders   cooking utensils
peg board

Teachers of preschool and kindergartens need to have collections of other objects which they can use for mathematical ends. Such collections would include:

shells of many sizes,   stones
shapes and colors   cutlery
beads of several varieties   hoops
cups and saucers   buttons of many sizes
balls   and colors
acorns   pipe cleaners, etc.
clay and modelling clay

SUMMARY

We think enough has been said to show that the child's environment is rich in objects and experiences which, with the help of an understanding teacher, can provide him with mathematical insight at his appropriate level of development. It has been said a number of times that this insight does not come about in a sterile environment. Some of our classrooms, unfortunately, are sterile. It is the teacher's responsibility to create a learning environment which, by the sheer power of the attraction of the exciting things to do in it, to explore, to experiment with, to come to manipulate and understand, will lead the child to become active in his learning. No mathematics program for young children should rely solely on a predetermined curriculum, for much of the worthwhile mathematics in the early learning years arises out of the everyday experiences of the children. But in order for these experiences to be worthwhile mathematically, the teacher has to be ready to capitalize on them and to have at hand a wide variety of means.

A vital component of curriculum making is that teachers themselves do the planning, yet always with knowledge of their children. In view of what she knows of her young children, each teacher must consider what concepts and experiences she hopes to introduce her children to in the course of her contact with them, and the ways best suited to introduce them. She will subordinate any program to the individual and be able to make the most use of those teachable moments which arise many times during the day in the classroom.

BIBLIOGRAPHY

Gans, Roma; Stendler, Celia; and Almy, Millie. *Teaching Young Children*. Yonkers-on-Hudson, New York: World Book Co., 1952.

Leeper, Sarah; Dales, Ruth; Skipper, Dora; and Witherspoon, Ralph. *Good Schools for Young Children*, 2d ed. New York: The Macmillan Co., 1968.

Rogers, Vincent R. "The New Mathematics." In *Teaching in the British Primary School*, Chapter 8. London: The Macmillan Co., 1970.

The Schools Council. *Mathematics in Primary Schools*. Curriculum Bulletin Number 1. London: Her Majesty's Stationery Office, 1969.

Tarnay, Elizabeth D. *What Does the Nursery School Teacher Teach?* Bulletin Number 106. New York: National Association for the Education of Young Children, 1965.

CHAPTER SIX

The Development of an Understanding of Science in the Child's Environment

When we talk about a child's science environment we are thinking about all those living and nonliving things in his world which he is forever eager to learn about. Often in the past teachers of early childhood have limited what children study in science to animals and plants, people, pets, insects and birds. They have talked about animals—the parts of the animals' bodies, what they eat, their habits, and their similarities with plants—and they have talked about plants and their functions—but only superficially, and they have seldom linked their lessons to any thematic planning which could extend the child's knowledge beyond merely superficial descriptions. Teachers need to remember that nowdays, with the impact of various media as stimulators, young children have much wider interests, are much more knowledgeable and are capable of much greater learning than we sometimes give them credit for.

What is science to the young child? In answering this question we have found the A.C.E.I. booklet *Young Children and Science* to be most helpful. This booklet considers science for the young child to be:

   . . . pausing to *wonder, reflect* and *speculate;*
   . . . *questioning* conditions and events around him;
   . . . *seeking* and *searching* for explanations;
   . . . *doubting* and *looking* for irregularities and deviations;
   . . . *seeking* and *verifying* information from reliable sources;
   . . . *sharing* ideas with others clarifying his thinking, raising questions and suggesting proposals for follow-up during discussions
   . . . *recording* his findings;
   . . . *organizing, interpreting, summarizing, generalizing* and *applying information.*[1]

[1] Reprinted from *Young Children and Science* by the Association for Childhood Education International (Washington, D.C.: Association for Childhood Education International, 1964), pp. 6-24 by permission.

We have said that young children are interested in many things and processes in their environment, some of which we can label scientific. Most children come to school with a little background in science—some, even, with a good background of stimulating science experiences. It could safely be said that nearly every child would have had contact with plants and animals of some kind and should have some idea of weather and seasonal changes, of electricity, water, gas, automobiles. Nearly every child has been to a supermarket and has seen foodstuffs displayed. Such a background provides the basis upon which teachers can build an interesting program of environmental studies in science. Certainly the degree and depth of study will vary from child to child, for each child's background is an important influence in determining his interests and, to some extent, his involvement in learning and understanding natural and physical phenomena around him.

Often teachers are disturbed by what appears to be a child's inability to tell of his experiences and may think the child's background to be a limited one. But this might not be the case. A sensitive and understanding teacher will form bonds with her children which enable communication, other than verbal, to take place. Many children know much more than is realized, and about many more things. Fostering the child's ability and readiness to communicate is a basic task for teachers in nursery schools and kindergartens. It is our task not only to help young children understand their environment but to help them to tell about it in terms that have meaning for them.

We learn much about the ways in which children gain information by watching them in their explorations. They feel things with their fingers, their cheeks, their lips and even their tongues. A young child walking with an adult who touches a tree may also feel the tree. If the adult says "rough," the child may repeat "rough" and then go on to feel all of the trees and many other objects nearby to apply the same term to them. In his testing of the meaning of "rough," he discovers wide variations in roughness.

We need to provide opportunities for children to feel various things, such as scotch tape, friction tape, molasses, clay soil, sand, water, glass, wood and iron. They will observe that some are smooth, some dry, others wet, soft, hard, sticky, mushy and so on. Such experiencing may seem commonplace to adults, but through the sense of touch, children learn to observe and describe the properties of objects—their textures, shapes, and sizes.

One child's background may be much more limited than that of others. Perhaps he has had no previous opportunity to experiment with clay, water, mud and other liquids (food coloring, etc.). Nor has he dabbled with magnetism, bells, buzzers, or simple low voltage electric wiring; nor built model rockets and space ships; nor handled insects, animals, fish; nor had pets of his own; nor planted a garden and watched the flowers and vegetables growing. Many parents would consider these activities to be dangerous, or messy, or simply beyond their ability to accommodate. There are countless reasons why the background experiences of some children are limited and why it is difficult at times to get them to become *involved* in things. Those parents who send their young child to nursery school beautifully and expensively dressed may handicap *real* involvement with objects, forces and natural events. This should not, however, deter the teacher from providing those kinds of experiences which enable children to explore scientific phenomena within the range of their environment. Some parents need to be helped to see things differently, for as we said in the previous section on mathematics, a person cannot know about mud, sand, clay and the like and what can be done with them, if he never gets the chance to manipulate them freely or to experiment with them.

What do young children want to know about that is in the area science? Think of the many questions they ask:

How does electricity get into the house?

Where does the sun go to?

How do the colors get into the rainbow?

How do butterflies come from cocoons?

How does the wind blow?

Why do cicadas, snakes shed their skin?

Their curiosity is insatiable and their questions are neverending. How do teachers answer these questions? We could easily fall into the trap of becoming too adult, too scientific, with our answers. Have you ever tried to tell a four-year-old, for example, about electricity and how it is made and how it runs along the wires outside and into the house? Have you watched his face as you tell him? Yet we must answer his questions honestly. The teacher is forever asking herself how simple she can make complicated events or processes; how involved she can let young children get in experiments which could have a degree of danger in them.

Let us think of the broad interests which young children have and which provide many avenues for exploration and involvement in learning. The following content areas and ideas taken from *Young Children and Science* [2] raise questions which should indicate to the teacher ways of directing learning.

Living Things

How do the flowers eat so they can grow like me?
Were you born before I was? (to the teacher)
How do crabs breathe under water?
Do babies breathe inside the mommy?
Can a wing thing that flies really come out of my caterpillar? Will the caterpillar be all gone?
How do vitamins get in food?
How is a moth born out of a cocoon?
Do jellyfish go in rivers or lakes?
When things die, are they skeletons?
Are all snakes poisonous?
How do fish breathe?
Why do some flowers smell so nice?
How do apple seeds get out of the apple to make a tree?
Do all plants have seeds?
Does the tortoise have skin inside there? Is it hooked on to that hard shell so he can't get all of him out?
How could this little worm breathe if the dirt was all over him?
Which part grows into a baby chick? (examining broken egg)

Matter and Energy

How can the water in that one be hot and this one be cold?
But where did the sticky go? Is the egg part still in there? (sampled cookies after helping to make them)
How could those colors get in my bubble just like paint?
Can light go through clouds?
How come the air is in the sky and the moon is in the sky but the air doesn't get up to the moon?
How does electricity get into our houses?
How does water get into my house?
Why is the water tank on top of the hill?
What is the sun like?
How does the light get in the light bulb?
Do jet planes use gas?
How do you get electricity in a dry cell battery?
Does a helicopter have a jet motor?

_____

[2] Association for Childhood Education International, *Young Children and Science* (Washington, D.C.: Association for Childhood Education International, 1964-65), pp. 26-27. Reprinted by permission of the publisher.

What makes a cork float?
What is fire made of?
How can it (cymbal) sing all by itself?
What makes some sounds so loud?
Are magnets sticky?

Earth

Where did my rain puddle go? Could the wind blow it away?
Where does the wind go when it stops blowing me?
Does that fog go all the way up to hide the sun?
Why can't the green leaves blow down? (collecting fallen leaves)
How could the rain stay up there all that other time when it didn't
  come down like now?
How does the Earth keep on turning?
How does gravity keep us from falling off the Earth?
If you can't go through it, how do you know how far it is through
  the Earth?
What kind of rock is this?
Did this rock come from a volcano?
How did the streaks get in the rocks?
What are rocks made of?
What makes summer?
How does the water keep from spilling off our Earth if it moves
  round and round?
Is it hot under the ground? Why?
Where did the oceans come from?
Where does an earthquake come from?
Why is the sky blue?
What makes steam?
What keeps a glider in the air?
What is wind?
What are clouds?

Beyond Earth

Does the Earth go around the sun?
How long does it take to go around the sun?
Why do you see the moon in the daytime?
Why can't you see stars in the daytime?
Could the sun melt the Earth if it came close?
Why does the moon look large and then small?
How far away is the moon?
Is the moon farther away than the sun?

How do they know what it is like on the moon when nobody
   has been there?*
How do they get pictures of the moon?
Do the planets have oceans?
Is it hot on Mars?
How do astronauts talk to people on Earth?
What does Telstar do?
Why does the moon have craters?
Are jet trails scratches on the sky?
Are there people on other planets?
Can astronauts chew food while they are in space?
Why doesn't the space capsule fall down?
Is the moon smaller than the Earth?
Why is it black in space?

How do young children learn about their science environment? Children are much less able than are adults to learn about their environment from words. They must experience it, experiment with things and ideas, and just mess about with it. Perhaps the following commentary best illustrates how the young child learns what things are, how they work, what they are for and how *he can use them for his own ends.* The commentary should indicate to the teacher what her role could be in facilitating learning.

Learning from a Hose

How much does a child learn sitting on the steps while you wash the car or sluice off the sidewalk? The sounds; more or less in a certain place; what you tell him about what you are doing—making the car clean, washing the dirt off the sidewalk. He will be able to go in and tell mother what you did, where you did it, what results you claim you got. But let him hold the hose himself, with the water running good and strong. What does he learn?

The jet effect of the stream of water, the hose pushing back in his hands.

What goes up must come down.

Safe places and unsafe places to shoot the stream of water.

People don't like being squirted.

He can make rain.

Water can hurt, can hit hard, can cause pain.

---

*This is no longer true, for we know that man has walked on the surface of the moon. This fact has led to more and more questions by children about the moon.

Water in a pan is static. Water from the hose has force and power, and he can control it to an extent. He can aim it so it will hit the garage roof, so it will hit the side of the house or splash back on him from the wall.

It cools the air.

By the way it sounds, it shows him where the sidewalk is, where the grass is, whether it is hitting the siding or the window on the house, when it hits the tree.

How to let him hold the hose and not learn something else:

If you get wet, you'll get a cold.

You'll get water in the window if you turn it toward the house.

You'll get people wet and they won't like you.

Don't turn it toward your face, it might hurt you. You'd get it up your nose and choke.

You'll make a muddy spot and get dirty. Save oh save my grass!

A child is afraid of nothing until danger is defined. Parents' fear will make him fearful. Any play surrounded by too much caution is only a source of anxiety.

1. Do the best job you can of making the surroundings relatively safe.

2. Trust nothing will happen until it does.

3. Don't judge your child's skill by your own awkward efforts blindfolded. You have spent a lifetime disregarding four of your five senses.[3]

Adults know all these things but children have to learn them. It is easy for the adult to think of the child as just playing around. So he is, in a way. Yet play which leads a child to knowledge of the properties and behavior of what *to us* are familiar things and processes is truly educative. And it is indispensable in the approach to what we adults call science.

If children are to ask useful questions about their natural environment and to search for answers, they must have direct experiences of phenomena. It is much better for children to handle and examine for themselves a snail or a magnet than to look at a picture, listen

---

[3] Reprinted with permission from T. D. Cutsforth, "Learning from a Hose," in *Water, Sand, and Mud as Play Materials*, pp. 14-15 (Washington, D.C.: National Association for Education of Young Children, 1959). Copyright © 1959 by the National Association for the Education of Young Children, 1834 Connecticut Avenue, N.W. Washington, D.C. 20009.

to someone's description, or just watch someone else. Teachers must provide opportunities for children to explore the nature and behavior of living and nonliving objects and materials.

For example, to answer the question "How do we know the wind is blowing?" children can observe the movement of leaves on trees, take a wind-vane outdoors each day to see in what direction the arrow points, and just stand out-of-doors to feel the moving air. The child's question may not be completely answered, but through these experiences he is developing the concepts: wind is moving air; sometimes the air moves fast and sometimes air moves slowly.

Guidance and discussion are extremely important in the introduction of ideas that can help children search for explanations. Exploring objects, such as the hose mentioned earlier, helps the young child to learn many more things about them than merely what they are commonly used for. Children should be encouraged to find other, perhaps novel, things to do with them. This is creative teaching, but in order for this to happen, the children must have many chances to observe and to experiment with the same objects or phenomena. The key phrase in developing concepts about science in young children in nursery and kindergarten is OBSERVATION and EXPERIMENTATION aided by an understanding teacher who assists the children to gain meaning from their observing and experimenting.

For the young child the study of science is the study of material objects and perceivable processes rather than of abstract ones. Emphasis should be placed on both the properties and functions of objects. The example given, "Learning From a Hose," is applicable here. Children should have a wide variety of first hand experience in grouping objects into classes and observing interactions between objects. Careful observing, accurate describing, and systematic ordering of materials and events are important science experiences.

The child's first contacts with objects of the environment are in his home and local community. in rural areas children have contact with a rich variety of living and nonliving objects. Alert, curious children learn a great deal from observations and interactions within that environment, but their observations may have more meaning if they have the guidance of sensitive, resourceful parents and teachers.

How can the teacher help children discover the "science" in their environment? First: the teacher has to know the interesting events to look for in the child's environment. She then needs to be aware of the value of timing; that is, to know the appropriate moment to draw the child's attention to whatever it is she wants him to become aware of. For example, if the teacher wants her children to observe changes in the weather and how at times the sky indicates or reflects these changes, then it would be good teaching to draw the children's attention to this when any change in the sky occurs during the school day, not just in a previously timetabled lesson. Walks around the school playground provide numerous opportunities for "discovering" things in their natural habitat. The success of teaching in this way relies on the teacher knowing what is, or could be there, and where to find it. Children should be taken frequently on walks and rambles so as to become familiar with the variety of living and nonliving things in their immediate surroundings.

Second: the teacher can help children to discover their environment by encouraging them to collect specimens of objects existing in their environment. Collections of objects such as shells, stones, leaves, grasses, plants, seeds, are all objects which individually have

A Child Engaged in a Natural Science Experiment in the Woods

similarities and at the same time many differences—of size, color, shape, weight, texture, hardness, fragrance, structure, function, and many more—and help the child to understand his world and nature.

Third: teachers can help children to organize their findings by guiding them in the sorting of their collections according to some pattern. The pattern the teacher sets would be one which best aids

Children Sorting out Their Findings from Science Experiments with the Help of the Teacher

understanding. A collection of leaves, for example, could be grouped in several ways: according to their size, color, shape or texture, whether or not they come from the same or different trees. The labels chosen should be of words suggested by the children. These words may be smooth, brown, sticky, bumpity, scratchy, hard, soft. A chart could be made to list words descriptive of texture, size, shape, color. The children themselves should suggest the number of groups, and the words used, but as always with the guidance of a sensitive teacher who understands that children use their senses "differently" from adults and may not feel, smell or see what the adult does.

It should be remembered that the displaying of collections should be artistically done for the concomitant learning in the aesthetics is important for children. Labels should be clear, with good quality printing. Backgrounds of colored cloth or paper will add to the effectiveness of the display.

Fourth: teachers should be familiar with books about science, and either have a personal collection or know where to obtain them. There are many books suitable for use with the four-, five-and six-year-olds which tell in pictures and simple story much about natural science. Other books, such as the Time/Life series *International Wildlife Encyclopedia,* are good classroom resource books to which the children as well as the teacher can refer. Children enjoy stories of animals and many of these stories become firm favorites which are asked for over and over again. A short bibliography of science books is given at the end of this chapter.

Fifth: the teacher should establish a *Science Table* or a *Science Corner* as a part of the learning environment. Such a place, to be alive, must be used freely by teacher and children. It should be everchanging. Children should be encouraged to bring objects from out-of-doors and from home to share with the class. The teacher needs to establish the idea that seeking, finding out, then sharing is important in her classroom. Many young children are eager to bring things into the classroom, but others will need to be encouraged, and indeed urged, to do so. With children in the latter group teachers will find their endeavors unrewarding at first; hence the necessity to *urge* and to incite children to hunt and to search for things. The teacher must set the example by bringing new and interesting specimens into the classroom regularly—even every day. Careful planning around a central theme which frequently includes rambles around the immediate school area, stimulates the "gathering" impulse of children. Discussions on and around the central theme and on specimens brought in by the teacher to initiate interest in the theme help stimulate children's thinking. Questions such as: "Have you anything like this at home? Will you ask Mommy if you can bring it to show us?", also help to get things going. Once begun, and with continuous teacher encouragement, the children usually will be eager to participate in sharing ideas and objects.

Sixth: the teacher can help children discover what is around them by conducting *field trips* to specially selected places. Such field trips need to be thoroughly well planned, with a preparation period and then a follow-up period. Both the pre- and post-periods are needed if the experience is to be effective as a learning experience. Think, for example, of taking the children on a field trip to the nearest zoo. Some suggested activities for a *preschool* class in preparation for the field trip could include:

1. Collecting pictures of zoo animals—displaying, naming and discussing;

2. Reading stories about animals and zoos (authentic, not fantasy stories);

3. Having picture reference books handy for children to look at;

4. Encouraging children to paint their favorite animals and to make up stories about them;

5. Modelling animals in playdough;

6. Singing songs and saying poems about animals—for example:

THE ZOO SONG

(F. N. E.)

7. Enacting in dance-drama some stories of animals, walking, crawling, running, springing, etc., as the animals do.

Some suggested activities for follow-up after the field trip could include:

8. Learning stories, songs and poems about the animals they saw and which impressed them most;

9. Constructing papier mache models of animals;

10. Building a sand-tray model of the zoo;

11. Painting animals and making up stories;

12. Dancing and drama.

Many stories are available about the animals they will see, and these should be read to the children. They should pay particular attention to the animals they are keeping in the classroom—gerbils, guinea pigs, etc.

The kindergarten class could include all the above activities and add language experience activities in reading, especially when connected with their art work. Stories about their paintings should be written by the teacher, read and displayed. A creative, thinking teacher will see many possibilities for learning in the preparation and in the follow-up of any field trip.

RECORDING CHILDREN'S SCIENCE

One purpose of any recording is to enable the child to recall what he has learned. Recording to the young child is pictorial and oral. He records his experiences in his art and craft work—in what he draws and what he makes. As his art forms much of the basis for his language development, another kind of recording can be brought into use similar to the methods used in the language experience learnings approach to reading. The teacher, going by what the child *says* about his experiences, writes some of this down. Together with the painting and modelling, the written language forms effective recording at the five- and six-year-old level. This simple writing also assists in the development of vocabulary.

In the kindergarten the child's art work and the teacher's writing of the child's description of what he has done can be combined in several ways. First the teacher can add a statement to the child's painting and then display it on the wall. Or several paintings and the stories about each can be stapled together to form a class or group book about an experience. Another way would be for groups of children to work together on a mural depicting aspects of the class or group experience. Photographs taken by the teacher can be still another way of recording children at work. Photographs afford children the opportunity for much later discussion of happenings and what they did.

MATERIALS WHICH WILL HELP THE YOUNG CHILD UNDERSTAND HIS ENVIRONMENT

We have said before that learning cannot take place in a vacuum and that the more stimulating the environment the more effective the learning. One condition for a stimulating environment is a wealth and variety of material in the classroom—material which challenges children to want to find out more about it; to ask what makes it "tick", what can be done with it. These "why's" and "wherefore's" are the foundations of the child's science.

Wherever possible science material should be real objects and not imitations. Illustrations and pictures, for example of animals, can stimulate much thinking and discusson by children but they should be used in conjunction with the real things wherever possible. All science material in the classroom should be safe for children's use and be placed for storage and display in accessible places. Such material would include as a minimum the following objects, animals and plants. The thinking teacher will add to this list as necessary to cope with the everchanging interests in her classroom. It should be remembered that most material can be used for science, irrespective of its original "purpose." Much of the mathematical material, for example, has scientific value.

Basic material would include:

Animals: Gerbils in a wire cage
Guinea Pigs
Rabbits
Hamsters
Fish (goldfish and tropical fish in a tank properly aerated. Some fish can survive in a tank not aerated.)
Chickens (hatched in a small incubator)

Plants: Geraniums in pots (geraniums flower all the year)
Cactus in pots
Household plants suitable to the area and which grow well indoors
Sweet potato growing in a glass jar filled with water
Seeds germinating (for observation and for later planting outdoors if possible)

Gardening Tools: Spades, rakes, hoes, small spades for pot-plant use, watering cans
Germinating boxes for seedlings
Containers for pot plants (milk cartons, plastic ice-cream or butter containers etc.)

Apparatus for Physical Science Exploration:
Scales, weights, measures—material from the math corner
Thermometers for indoors and outdoors
Soils, sand, rocks, shells
Magnifying glasses of several sizes
Magnets and simple electrical circuits, batteries, flashlights
Plastic containers of various sizes
Pots and pans for flotation and for other water play
Observation boxes (for the observing of insects, spiders, etc.)
Things from the kitchen to taste and smell
Cooking apparatus—electric skillet, hot-plate
Things for the touch-table (textures, colors, sizes, shapes)

The quest for a better understanding of the world in which we live is characteristic of young children. It is neverending, and the answers that are found are tentative rather than final. Part of the fascination of science in a child's environment lies in this quest itself. If children can savor some of this excitement as they strive for better understanding, they will have had important experiences in science that will be of first class value when they are introduced to the more highly organized, abstractly-ordered sciences.

BIBLIOGRAPHY

Gans, Roma; Stendler, Celia; and Almy, Millie. "The Child as Scientist." In *Teaching Young Children,* Chapter 10. Yonkers-on-Hudson, New York: World Book Co., 1952.

Heffernan, Helen, and Todd, Vivian E. "The Child Enters His Scientific World" and "Understanding Space and Quantity." In *The Kindergarten Teacher,* Chapters 9 and 10. Boston: D.C. Heath & Co., 1960.

Hill, Patty Smith. *Kindergarten.* Reprint by Association for Childhood Education International, 3615 Wisconsin Avenue, N.W., Washington, D.C. 20016, 1967.

Hymes, James L., Jr. *Teaching the Child under Six,* 2d ed. Columbus, Ohio: Charles E. Merrill Publishing Co., 1974. (Science is included in chapters throughout the book.)

Leavitt, Jerome E., and Salot, Lorraine. "Science." In *The Beginning Kindergarten Teacher*, Chapter 12. Minneapolis, Minnesota: Burgess Publishing Co., 1965.

Leeper, Sarah; Dales, Ruth; Skipper, Dora; and Witherspoon, Ralph. "Science." In *Good Schools for Young Children*, Chapter 14. New York: The Macmillan Co., 1968. (Includes discussions of objectives, characteristics of a good program, how to teach science, etc.)

Read, Katherine H. "Intellectual Perception and Mastery." In *The Nursery School: A Human Relationships Laboratory*, Chapter 13. Philadelphia: W.B. Saunders Co., 1966.

Rogers, Vincent R. "The New Science." In *Teaching in the British Primary School*, Chapter 9. London: The Macmillan Co., 1970.

Wellem, Vander Eyken. "In Search of Intellectual Development." In *The Preschool Years*, Chapter 9. Baltimore: Penguin Books, A Penguina Special Edition, 1967.

Science Books with Various Activities and Investigations

Anderson, Devito, et al. *Developing Children's Thinking through Science.* Englewood Cliffs, New Jersey: Prentice-Hall, Inc., 1970.

Association for Childhood Education. *Young Children and Science.* Washington, D.C.: Association for Childhood Education, 1965.

Carin, Arthur A., and Sund, Robert B. *Teaching Science through Discovery,* 2d ed. Columbus, Ohio: Charles E. Merrill Publishing Co., 1970.

Cox, Louis T., Jr. *Working with Kindergarten Children in Science.* Towson, Maryland: State Teachers College, 1959.

Greenlee, Julian. *Teaching Science to Children.* Dubuque, Iowa: William C. Brown Co., 1957.

Karplus, Robert, and Their, Herbert. *A New Look at Elementary School Science.* Chicago: Rand McNally & Co., 1967.

Sheckles, Mary. *Building Children's Science Concepts through Experiences with Rocks, Soil, Air, and Water.* New York: Columbia University Teacher's College Bureau of Publications, 1958.

Sund, Robert B.; Trowbridge, Leslie W.; Tillery, Bill W.; and Olson, Kenneth V. *Elementary Science Teaching Activities: A Discovery Laboratory Approach.* Columbus, Ohio: Charles E. Merrill Publishing Co., 1967.

Journal

Science and Children. National Science Teacher's Association. 1201 Sixteenth Street, N.W., Washington, D.C. 20036.

CHAPTER SEVEN

The Development of an Understanding of the Child's Social Environment

The young child coming into a school setting at age four or five finds himself in a very different world from that of his home. This is particularly so of the child coming from a home environment which is warm and understanding. Up till this stage his parents, especially his mother, have played the most significant role in developing his social awareness. Now the preschool and kindergarten teacher assumes some of the socializing role that has hitherto been the responsibility especially (but not solely) of the parents. For some children this break with their parents can be traumatic; however, much of the trauma can be avoided if teacher and mother and child are able to establish a mutually cooperative and supportive relationship. Such a relationship will help to reassure the child that he is not alone among the 20 or 30 seeking the attention and approval of one adult, the teacher.

Some children will need more reassurance than others, and a few may not so much need as try to demand continual attention. The first few days of an entering group can be very demanding of the teacher, and call for every ounce of her kindliness, common sense and firmness. It will help the teacher if she says to herself from time to time that she is not just bearing up as well as she can in a wearing situation but helping these children learn to share and contribute while they are learning to cope with the problems and opportunities arising in this new society. Thus they are undergoing a very valuable part of their socializing education.

It is, therefore, important that the child's, each child's, first teacher become his friend, who will give him sympathetic guidance and comfort when needed, and who will set comprehensible boundaries and limits for him and his peers. In this way a child's first encounter with a new aspect of his society will be supportive and encouraging. We know that a child who fears is not likely to venture far into the unknown. He should not be fearful in his new environment; the positive supportive classroom atmosphere which we have mentioned frequently in this book is very important to the child.

Early schooling provides the young child with the companionship of children his own age. He quickly becomes one of a group, for better or worse depending on factors—the attitude of his teacher toward him, for example—no longer under his control. He is still basically egocentric in nature. He has to learn to live with others similarly egocentric, and this is no small task nor is it something which happens in a short time.

There is no one way to help children become social beings. The teacher must always look to the individual child as the starting point. Teachers have used stories about great people as a means of inculcating desired moral behavior. Frequently, these stories place the great person in a situation where he has to choose between two opposing modes of behavior: one right and moral and the other undesirable. Such stories which have a "moral" ending to them are of questionable value to the young child as teaching situations for the "moral" is not always obvious to him. Each child takes from his experience what he wants and at his level of comprehension. The success of any teaching hinges on whether or not he sees the experience as being important to him.

Some teachers who outwardly give the appearance of being kind and gentle (those teachers who say "You know you mustn't do that for Miss X doesn't like it!", and leave it at that without the child *understanding* why the behavior is disliked) work in a negative way towards helping children become more socially mature in their classroom. Their control is external to the child, not internal. This is apparent when someone else takes over the group in the teacher's absence and notes how little self direction there is among the children.

A positive, accepting atmosphere in the classroom is a crucial factor in fostering independence. Most children enter kindergarten at the age of five, or close to it. Children of this age are mature enough to begin working in small groups. After a few weeks of school, they should begin to organize their own games. For example, the auditory discrimination games on pages 60-61 lend themselves to this approach. A degree of cooperation will be generated and if nurtured will increase as the children get to know and learn to respect one another. There are many other curriculum experiences which, if guided skilfully by the teacher, will give children the opportunity to organize for themselves. Art murals where children first discuss and undertake to work each on a certain part are good sharing experiences which foster cooperation. Small group discussions where the children take turns, listen and ask one another questions are also valuable.

**Children Engaged in Group Activities with
Displays of their Work in the Background**

In guiding the children towards independence the teacher should not expect too much too soon. If at the end of first term groups are beginning to function independently, then much progress has been made.

Probably the social act of *sharing* is one of the most difficult things for a young child to grasp. How he "shares" depends largely on his previous home background and the attitude of his family. Sharing the attention of the teacher is difficult for the insecure child who needs constant reassuring. It is obvious that a teacher with 20 or so children has to do her best to share her time with all of her children as they need it. The sharing of one's "best friend" is difficult for many children of this age. Retorts such as "We don't want to play with you!" made by two firm (for the time being) buddies are frequently heard in the classroom.

How does the teacher help her children come to grips with their social world? We have been indicating thus far that the beginnings of an understanding by the child of his place in his society must be with the child himself and with his relationship with his peers in his new classroom environment. If such an understanding is to be growth-building, the child should feel *positive* about himself and his relationships with others. In other words he feels happy to be at school and is able to interact with others. The teacher helps by lessening the strangeness of the new environment. The new ways of doing things, the new routines, ways of disciplining, must be introduced gradually and be accepted and as far as possible understood by the child.

The understanding teacher sees the great value in play as an avenue for socialization. Play in the preschool and kindergarten will not be as spontaneous as the play that arises between friends in their home environment. This is due to many factors. A school class is too large a group to be, for the child, a social unit. Then there is the teacher, always there, always supervising, or likely to. In the preschools and kindergartens today it is not unusual to find children coming from various localities. Few children have contact with others in their class when the school day is over. In the preschool and kindergarten, then, friendships have to be formed and this, in itself, takes time. The physical environment of the preschool or kindergarten is new and strange and until it becomes familiar there may be a noticeable reserve in the play of the children. The development of a secure atmosphere, one in which friendships can arise and flourish, will in time promote play of the best kind, free and spontaneous play.

Another sharing trial for young children is the sharing of time. Some children simply cannot wait their turn to get something, to work in an area with favorite material etc. Children do have preferences for material and activities and want the preferred activity when they want it. Teachers need to be prepared for this behavior, even to having extra supplies of material on hand. It is no good saying, in effect, "Your turn will come later." When the material for an exciting activity is too limited, problems of sharing occur and the teacher is faced with difficulties.

The reader should refer to Part One of this book and to the section on "Play in the Socialization of the Child" (p. 10) for a detailed discussion of play. It is sufficient to repeat here that teachers foster play for they see its importance in the development of the child's total personality.

What we are attempting to say here is that when the young child begins to find security in his school environment, he is able to be more acceptant of other children in this common environment. He gains this security, this feeling of self-worth mainly through the way other people react to him and to what he does. And the most important person in his new environment is his teacher.

TEACHERS AND THEIR TASK

How can the teacher provide the child with the right kinds of social experiences? By "right kinds" of experiences we mean those which aid his independency and foster his individuality. It is so important, especially with preschool children, that the number of children in the group be small, not more than twenty children (four-year-olds) with a teacher and an aide. Once the numbers get above this, regimental practices begin and as we know the more regimented the classroom the less stress is placed on individuality and independency. There are still many teachers, for example, who systematically line all the children up at given times each day for visits to the toilet. Who says all children want to visit the toilet between 10.15 A.M. and 10.30 A.M.? Do not practices such as this require children to conform before they are really able? For some children, who come from very understanding homes where sensible flexibility is fostered, conforming to certain kinds of group patterning of behavior such as the example given of toilet training is in opposition to their developing self-reliance.

From an understanding of the immediate environment of the classroom teachers move the thinking and experiencing of the children into the outside world. Young children are fascinated by other people and what they do, especially those people with heroic (for the child) occupations such as:

the fireman
the milkman
the policeman
the bus driver
the man at the supermarket
the bakerman
the ambulance driver
the pilot of an airplane
the nurse, the doctor and the dentist
the farmer

It will depend to a great extent on the location of the preschool or kindergarten as to how these interesting people and their occupations can be introduced to the children. It might be convenient for the baker to come into the classroom (in baker's clothing of course) and be with the children for a while. If he then could invite the children to the bakery to watch the bread being baked this would be a good experience for the children. Firemen are a good standby and are always ready to oblige young children. Could a visit to an airport be arranged with the aid of a pilot and the children being allowed to climb into a plane (no matter how small)? Think of the supermarket manager taking the children through his exciting store. There are many avenues for exploring the neighborhood and learning about it from people the children are, in some ways, acquainted with. Field trips are essential and so much interest can be aroused and maintained through preparatory and follow-up activities.

There are many other social experiences which the children can be involved with. A general theme of "Helping Other People" can be developed. Who can we help? One group of young children we know in Florida has "adopted" an old people's home and regularly visits with the senior citizens who live there. This has been a rewarding activity for both children and the old people, for new and meaningful relationships have developed. Other themes might be "What can we do to help keep our country a good place to live in?" "What can we do to overcome prejudice?" This question is always a difficult one for teachers of the very young to handle for the prejudice they are dealing with in their children is the prejudice of the children's parents and other family members.

From time to time the teacher has to cope with problems which may have strong emotional overtones. A child in the group or a parent may die. Generally there is at least one child in each group who has a special physical or mental or emotional handicap. Such children while requiring "special" care in one respect should be made to feel one of the group and not be obviously singled out for special attention. Usually the children in the group readily accept the child and his handicap and make little fuss of it. It is the friendless, withdrawn or aggressive child who causes the teacher most concern and who proves to be the most difficult to help become more acceptable in the social group. Here the understanding teacher works patiently with each child gradually bringing him into group activities in a way which will give him support from the group. There is no one way of doing this for it is a matter of the interplay between the personalities of each group—of the teacher, the children, the "special" child—and the situation as it arises.

SUMMARY

We do not teach "Social Studies" to four- and five-year-old children. Rather, the emphasis is on personal social development. There is a difference here. The latter cannot be acquired from a book nor developed from any sequence of prescribed lesson plans. It is the result of a child interacting with his environment. We have tried to emphasise that for the preschool and kindergarten child, it is so necessary that they enjoy a secure environment, secure from fear and undue pressures to perform and conform. Yet this same environment must challenge the child in every possible way, socially and intellectually. He needs to experience successes and learn how to handle failures.

We have said too, that the understanding teacher respects her children as individuals with their own unique personalities, tempos of working and thinking, and levels of maturity. When introducing children to their first experience with "organized" schooling, it is important that they understand what is expected of them. A too adult-directed environment allows little scope for individual growth. On the other hand an environment which is lacking direction and in which the children are aimless is just as restricting. And so a balance between freedom and direction must be striven for by each teacher.

BIBLIOGRAPHY

Association for Childhood Education International. *Parents—Children—Teachers*. Bulletin Number 28A. Washington, D.C. Association for Childhood Education International, 1969.

Ambrose, Edna, and Miel, Alice. *Children's Social Learning*. Washington, D.C.: Association for Supervision and Curriculum Development, 1958.

Ashton-Warner, Sylvia. *Teacher*. Baltimore: Penguin Books, 1963.

Brown, Mary, and Precious, Norman. *The Integrated Day in the Primary School*. London: Ward Lock Educational, 1968.

Cohen, Dorothy H, and Stern, Virginia. *Observing and Recording the Behavior of Young Children*. New York: Columbia University Teacher's College Press, 1958.

Gillham, Helen L. *Helping Children Accept Themselves and Others*. New York: Columbia University Teacher's College Bureau of Publications, 1959.

Gordon, Ira J. *Children's View of Themselves.* Washington, D.C.: Association for Childhood Education International, 1942.

Hill, Patty Smith. *Kindergarten.* Washington, D.C.: Association for Childhood Education International, 1942; reprint.

Isaacs, Susan. *The Children We Teach,* 2d ed. London: University of London Press, 1965.

Miel, Alice, and Kiesler, Edwin. *The Short-Changed Children of Suburbia.* New York: Institute of Human Relations Press, 1967.

Redl, Fritz. *Understanding Children's Behavior.* New York: Columbia University Teacher's College Bureau of Publications, 1949.

Rogers, Vincent R. *Teaching in the British Primary School.* London: The Macmillan Co., 1970, Chapter 3.

Winnicott, D.W. *The Child, the Family, and the Outside World.* Hammondsworth, England: Pelican Books, 1964.

PART THREE

The Child and His Curriculum

In many ways the underlying philosophy which determines the kind of curriculum in preschools and in kindergartens is the same. One must remember that children entering kindergarten at five years of age are one or two years older than nursery school children and therefore some are capable of more sustained effort than are the younger children. However, one must constantly remember that children vary greatly in ability, and a four-year-old nursery school child may be working at a level above that of many kindergarten children.

A curriculum, be it for a preschool or kindergarten, must be developed to meet the needs of the particular group of children the teacher has at that time. As the composition of groups change, individual interests and abilities will change. A good curriculum will be everchanging.

The following principles regarding curriculum construction are common to both preschools and kindergartens:

1. Children learn most effectively by becoming involved in self-chosen experiences from a broad framework of experiences carefully planned by the teacher.
2. Children need to become involved in ongoing centers of interest.
3. Children need the guidance and support of an empathetic teacher who constantly strives to mold the curriculum to meet the individual needs of the children under her care.
4. Children need opportunities for individual work.
5. Children need the experience of working in small groups.
6. Children need to experience all facets of a well planned curriculum.
7. In their social interaction with others children need opportunities for spontaneous play both indoors and out-of-doors.

8. An integrated approach to curriculum design best suits the learning patterns of young children. This approach is contrasted with a subject-centered approach which sees learning in a more adult-oriented way.

THE ROLE OF THE TEACHER

The role of the teacher in preschool and kindergarten is diverse. She must:

1. Have a sound knowledge of child growth and development;
2. Have clearly defined objectives and work systematically towards achieving them;
3. Work to obtain a deep insightful knowledge of each child under her care;
4. Aim to help each child develop to his full potential;
5. Be responsible for developing and maintaining a stimulating, challenging environment;
6. Be capable of inspiring children to give of their very best at all times;
7. Be perceptive, to anticipate the needs of the children and to capitalize on the "teachable moment" as it arises;
8. Be ready to provide help and guidance when it is needed;
9. Be able to evaluate the efforts and achievements of individual children;
10. Keep appropriate records of the individual progress of each child.

INTEGRATED DAY

We have accepted the current term "The Integrated Day" to describe how we see a normal day in operation in an early childhood classroom. The basis of an integrated day is correlation; the bringing together of things which go together.

We believe this is the way the young child sees his world and learns about it. The opposite of this is, of course, fragmentation. In Section B of Part Two, discussing the child's environment, we implied that subjects as taught in schools are intellectually sophisticated systems of knowledge. The young child, for example, even though he knows a good deal about spaces and directions and movements from place to place, does not and cannot know geography. The same argument can be applied to other subjects. Failure to appreciate clearly enough the great differences between the way a child grows to understand his environment and the way an adult has learned to understand *his* environment has led to that sad belief that the education of the child began with the introduction of school subjects.

When planning for an integrated approach to learning, it is to be remembered, however, that it is the child himself who does the integrating—not the teacher. The teacher can help by providing the child with materials and giving him opportunities to become involved in the right kinds of experiences, but ultimately it is the child who does the integrating, the grasping of the "whole" picture.

Basic also to an integrated day is interest. As we said earlier in Part One there must be pupil interest for real learning to take place. But when talking about the integrated day pupil interest should lead to pupil excitement. This indicates to us the kind of atmosphere that should exist in a classroom operating on the plan of an integrated day: an atmosphere of excitement.

An integrated day is a flexible day. If, as we know, children's interests rise and fall according to no known time sequence, then a classroom which fosters these interests and realizes the learning that can transpire from developing them must be flexible in order to accommodate them. The clue to flexibility lies in the teachers' knowledge that mathematics, language learning, social living, and other aspects of a child's development can be learned through most activities which arise as a result of her capitalizing on children's interests. Readers should refer to Chapter Five of Part Two and read the entries from a teacher's diary given on page 111 as examples of how learning occurs from developing children's interests. The teacher who integrates her day accepts children's interests when they arise, attempts to generate them into centers of interest and then gives some direction to the child's way of working through these interests.

So far we have said that the integrated day is first a unifying process of learning as opposed to a fragmented approach. Second, it capitalizes on the interests of the child and attempts to draw learning from a deeper study of such interests. Third, as a way of organizing classroom learning, it is an extremely flexible approach which has few of the constraints of the more "formalized" learning environment, especially regarding what to learn, when to learn it and how the learning should be done.

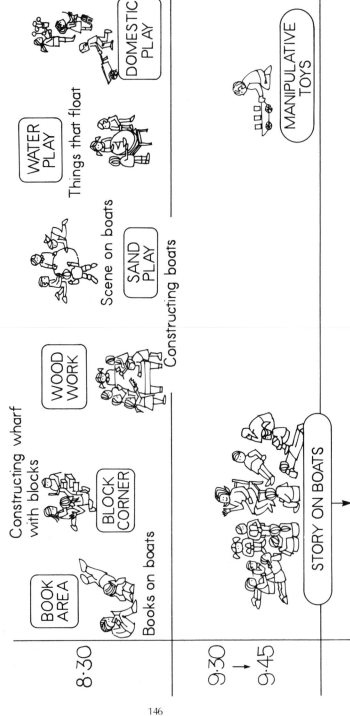

central theme BOATS

BOOK AREA
Books on boats

Constructing wharf with blocks

BLOCK CORNER

WOOD WORK

Scene on boats

SAND PLAY
Constructing boats

WATER PLAY
Things that float

DOMESTIC PLAY

MANIPULATIVE TOYS

STORY ON BOATS

8.30

9.30
↓
9.45

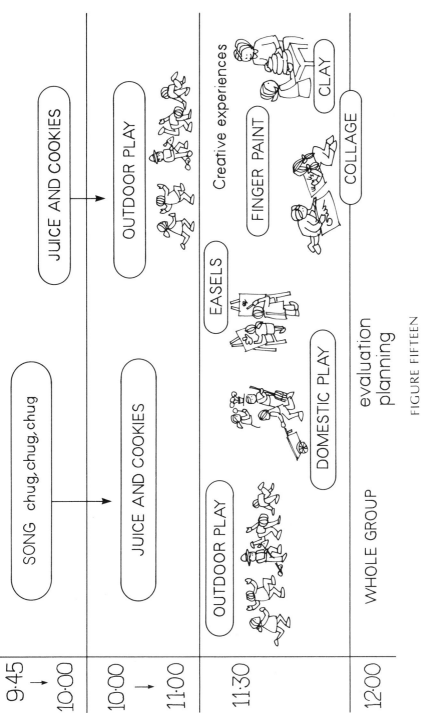

9.45 → 10.00	SONG chug, chug, chug
10.00 → 11.00	JUICE AND COOKIES
	OUTDOOR PLAY
	JUICE AND COOKIES
	OUTDOOR PLAY
11.30	Creative experiences
	EASELS
	FINGER PAINT
	CLAY
	DOMESTIC PLAY
	COLLAGE
12.00	WHOLE GROUP evaluation planning

FIGURE FIFTEEN

147

Throughout this book we have stressed that the classroom environment must be a stimulating one. This is especially important when operating an integrated approach to learning, for much of the child's interest is generated from within his classroom environment. This stimulus is very often what is physically present in the classroom and the attitude of the teacher to what is there. The classroom can be full of wonderful things to explore and to learn, yet little really may be done with it if the teacher cannot see its possibilities. The opposite of this can also be found—a bare room made alive by the teacher and children making, building and bringing things into it—things which are more than objects, things which have meaning. The role of the teacher here is obvious We have said before that learning does not take place in a vacuum and the teacher does not sit around waiting for learning to happen. Rather, she gets learning going, interests begun, then guides their development. But one always must remember that it is the *quality* of the experience the learner is having that is important in education.

In the nursery school and kindergarten there is little place for a tight, rigid daily timetable which allocates set times for certain subjects. We prefer the allocation of large blocks of time to self-chosen activities where children work at centers of interest. Small groups meet and come together at times as one whole group for common experiences such as discussion time or story time, music, movement and drama.

The daily plan of activities can best be diagrammed as in Figure Fifteen, and it should be noted that in this diagram we are showing *possible* groupings, regroupings and movement of children during the day. This kind of planning is flexible. While we recommend that the day should begin with children moving directly to areas and activities of their choosing as they come into the room, the day could begin with a whole group activity especially if something has aroused the interest of the whole class.

DAILY AND LONG-TERM PLANNING

We have, in several places throughout this book, stressed the need for adequate and suitable teacher planning. The need for such planning is obvious, for without it the activities of the children and their ensuing learning would lack direction. Some teachers might think that they can manage their class without adequate and detailed planning. With some teachers this practice is disastrous, but even experienced and capable teachers will do a much better job if they give more time to careful planning. What is planned should show that the children are working at tasks appropriate to the present stage in their development and the tasks are one of a series of experiences in a carefully planned sequence. We are suggesting here that no matter how experienced and successful the teacher might be, some planning is necessary to sound teaching, and learning, and that the more thought out the planning the more proficient should be the teaching.

All teachers need to have clearly established stages or levels of development of their children in their minds so as to be able to prescribe for each child. In addition, teachers need to have a reasonable idea of what they will accept as quality work from each child. This does not mean that each child will reach the same level of learning at the same time or at the same rate. But it does mean that the teacher *who has prescribed well for her children* can expect to receive, and in fact will only accept, the very best work from each child. We said earlier in this book in the discussion on mathematics that central to the whole problem of planning a systematic program is that the work must be well thought out in advance, be sequential in development and be adapted by the teacher to the needs of the individual child. Such preparation by the teacher is vital if she is to be able *to recognize learning when it occurs*—an important task with young children.

Long-term goals are generally those broadly stated goals which seek to further each child's all-round development. To achieve such goals it is essential that the teacher make an effort to diagnose the present stage of each child's development. She does this in many ways: through parent-teacher sharing of information about the child; by using selected standardized tests of ability and readiness; but above all by patient and systematic observation of the child's behavior in every situation in which he is involved in the classroom. A sound assessing of the stage of each child's development will assist the teacher to plan for experiences which will lead the child on to the next stage in his development.

Short-term goals are in many ways steps to long-term ones. They are, by their nature, more specific for they are dealing with smaller units of work which can be completed in a shorter time. Short-term units in curriculum planning for preschools and kindergartens can best be planned using the "Central Theme" approach. We have suggested this approach throughout our book. Well planned, it can be most effective as a guide to curriculum construction. It is particu-

**Long-Term Planning Is Essential for
Successful Nursery Accommodation**

larly appropriate for the kind of classroom practice which utilizes
an activity-centered approach to learning. As its name implies a
chosen theme becomes central to the activities of the children. It
cannot become the governing influence for *every* activity. This would
result in an extremely artificial curriculum and would cause teachers
to ignore other opportunities for learning which could not be linked
with the theme. For instance, much of the understanding of early

Math

- Discrimination
- Incidental counting
- Card games
  Number games

Language

- Pre-reading: sorting
- Language: displays of colors
- Building up community books
  on colors—extending to
  sentences
- Card games: e.g.
  "Which color is missing?"
  "Pass the Color."
- Describing games
- Language experience from
  other activities, e.g.
  cooking.

Nature

- Beginning a nature
  table featuring
  colors in nature
- Nature walk to
  nearby park.

COLORS

Cooking

- Colored popcorn
- Making cupcakes
  and cookies—
  frosting of
  various colors.

Creative

- Making "blocks" from
  milk cartons—paper
  tearing
- Play-dough with specific
  colors (children make
  own dough)
- Making of murals from
  stories read
- Paper-tearing mural
- Lumber crayon work
- Woodworking—making
  model and painting it

Sensory Discrimination

- Touch Table.

Music and Rhythm

- "The Red Red Robin" (song)
- "Lavender's Blue" (song)
- Rhymes dealing with
  walking, swaying,
  hopping
- Mime, e.g.
  "As small as a mouse."
  "As tall as a house."

FIGURE SIXTEEN

Central Theme: Colors (for Kindergarten)

number relationships is, as we said earlier in Chapter Five of Part Two, often difficult to link with every theme. A great deal of the meaningful mathematics learning in the early years is linked with those incidental situations which arise during the activities of the the day.

An example of planning using a central theme is diagrammed on page 151. Some teachers prefer to set out their planning in diagrammatic form, for it facilitates reading. The teacher should, however, compose a format which suits her. It should be remembered that, as we said before, not *all* the activities of the class can be directly linked to the theme, nor should they be linked. Forced linking makes a stilted program.

To elaborate on the theme in Figure Sixteen:

Color displays.   In areas of the room where certain colors are concentrated. Children should be encouraged to bring objects of various colors from home to add to the teacher's collections.

Modelling experiences.   Salt and flour dough, mixed by the children and vividly colored with food dyes could be the experience medium.

Nature experiences.   Children should be taken into a park or to the countryside to collect leaves, flowers, twigs, stones, etc., and classify them in the classroom according to colors. A display of color in nature should be begun in the science area.

Games.   These should aid visual discrimination (pre-reading) "Which color is missing?" (using sets of colored cards)

"The Postman" (delivering colored cards)

Cooking experiences.   (a) Popcorn – the colored variety. (b) Cupcakes or cookies with frosting of different colors.

Songs.   There are many suitable songs which mention colors. A song which can be linked to a discrimination exercise is:

> All the little color cards
> Sitting in a ring.
> Red cards, red cards
> Dance and sing.
> Tra la la la la, la la la la la
> La la la la la la la. etc.

Painting. Children mix own colors and discover how a new color will emerge from mixing two colors.

DAILY PLAN—COLORS		
	Kindergarten	
A. *Activities:*	1. Book Area:	Books on colors
	2. Block Corner:	Sorting and classifying blocks into colors and shapes. Building houses with colored blocks—making a street of houses.
	3. Sand Play:	Measuring and pouring sand into various sized containers.
	4. Cooking:	Making and frosting cupcakes. Preparing some language experience from this activity.
	5. Language Games:	"Snap" "Pass the Color".
B. *Sharing Time:*	1. Telling of activities related to cooking experience. Look at language stories.	
	2. Beginning of a color display— yellow.	
C. *Nature Time:*	Walk to the park (aim to observe colors in nature and to collect objects for use in classroom activities). Arranging a nature display upon return. Labelling of objects displayed.	
D. *Outdoor Play:*	Games and relaxation.	
E. *Story Time and Singing, etc.:*	"Red is Never, No Never a Mouse" (Story). "When the Red Red Robin Comes" (Song).	

Stories. "Red is Never, No Never a Mouse," "The Little Yellow Bird," "Hailstones and Halibut Bones," "Ann Likes Red," "The Little Blue Engine That Could."

A Daily Plan would be similar to the one diagrammed on page 151 (though this diagram specifically shows how *children* can group for activities). Using the central theme, "Colors," a daily plan *could* be as follows:

We must emphasize that this is only a *sample* daily plan. Each day should have some new activity and a fresh way of working at the tasks planned. Only the teacher who intimately knows her children can successfully plan for them. Some of our suggested activities for the planned day will not be used the following day. Similarly the activities A through E should vary. For example, it is unlikely that a nature walk would be planned for two days in succession. Some art and carpentry could be substituted here. The teacher, once she has thought out her theme in some detail and is cognizant of what she wants her children to experience during the time allocated for the development of the theme, can be flexible in her daily planning for she knows what she wants for her children.

CLASSROOM ORGANIZATION

The Physical Environment

INDOORS

Children need security and order in their lives. Security and order can be better achieved in a school setting where the children have become part of an environment which they helped to create and help to maintain. If the teacher is quietly insistent and consistent very quickly children learn, for example, that certain materials belong in certain places and that "tidy-up" time follows a time of work. The realization that one assists in the cleaning up in the classroom comes not through "tidy-up" periods at set times, at 10:00 A.M. each day for example, but rather by developing a sense of responsibility and a sense of pride in the child knowing that the classroom is his room.

The security that comes with a familiar environment is important for young children. While the environment remains familiar it must not, however, remain static; some new things need to happen daily. This keeps the children alert and active. Exciting kinds of play evolve as the result of an environment which is always stimulating. In this regard materials and equipment will change and be added to as the children grow and develop. The general structure of the room, however, should remain constant. Minor rearrangements will occur and children themselves will often initiate such changes. There is a danger in too sweeping changes in the arrangement of the classroom and children should not be constantly confronted with major room reorganization.

The classroom itself must provide adequate space for children to move about, exploring, discovering and experimenting, without feeling restricted or hemmed in by inadequate space. The recommended amount of indoor space per child is approximately 40 to 60 square feet. Activity areas should be sufficiently spaced out so as to avoid distractions from other areas. For example, block-building and carpentry work should be situated well away from the quieter activities.

Storage of equipment is another item to consider when planning the working space of a classroom. Adequate storage space for blocks, manipulative toys, and indeed all the material used in the room, is essential. As the children will be involved daily in the systematic packing up of materials, functional and accessible storage shelves are vital.

Classrooms for young children should always be situated on ground floor level. There should be sufficient windows for adequate natural lighting and fresh air. Walls should be tastefully painted with durable, washable paint. Large display areas should be available on the walls, and should be at a height suited to young children. Floors should be of material which can easily be maintained and cleaned. Carpeting on part of the floor is valuable for many of the class activities. It helps deaden a lot of the normal noise generated by a class full of youngsters, and as well as being warm in winter it allows for large group congregation. There should be provision for a "wet area" where water play, art activities and the like are done. The floor in this section is best covered in washable vinyl tile.

Furniture for the room should be light, durable and stackable. There are available today certain types of trapezoidal shaped tables which can be set up in varying functional arrangements depending on the particular activity at the time, and chairs are available to match. Some teachers also like to place small rocking chairs in the library corner in addition to scattering comfortable rugs on the floor. Sometimes the occasion arises where individual children or a small group may need to work on the floor. Provision should be made for this. In such instances tables can be temporarily stacked aside.

Actual room arrangement will depend on available facilities, furniture, room size and access to out-of-doors. Each teacher will have a preference with regard to her room organization. Adequate toilet facilities, preferably adjacent to the classroom, are essential. Fittings in the toilets should be child sized and at child level. Floor tiles should be of a variety which can be cleaned easily. A sink is necessary in or near the toilets for washing hands and for general cleanliness.

OUT-OF-DOORS

Outdoor play is as essential as indoor play, and the outdoor environment should be as exciting and stimulating as the indoor one. Children, when outdoors, will often give vent to pent-up feelings or will

Children Engaged in Outdoor Activity

just run for the thrill of running and being alive. For these reasons large open areas where children can run, jump and move are essential. Ideally the outdoor play area should be adjacent to the classroom so that children can move freely from one place to another.

(The housekeeping area is best placed with access to the out-of-doors. Often dramatic play will necessitate a "walk to the shop," "a trip to a beauty parlor" and so on. The children's interest will be sustained and imagination will often be stimulated if there is easy access to outside areas.)

Availability of staff for supervision of children is a consideration when defining boundaries for outside areas. All the outdoor area should be enclosed with a child-proof fence and gate which can be locked. This is essential with young nursery school children, who if given the opportunity, are likely to wander out on to the streets.

The outdoor area should be aesthetically pleasing. The grounds should include shade trees, green grass, cement paths, an area where the children can garden as well as an outdoor sand pit and water play area. If at all possible there should be areas in the grounds less developed where wildlife such as birds, insects, etc., may be observed in their natural surroundings.

Outdoor Play Equipment for a Children's Playground

Outdoor space must provide opportunities for active, vigorous play and this aspect of the curriculum as with other aspects must be carefully planned. Wise selection of outdoor equipment is essential. Inclusion of items such as swings and slides can present a safety hazard. In contrast, equipment such as climbing frames can be used with boards and rope ladders and stimulate unlimited constructive play.

The placement of equipment and material will be influenced by the actual site. Certain points, however, should be considered when arranging equipment. For example, all climbing equipment should be placed on soft surfaces such as grass or sand so as to lessen the impact if a child should fall. Tricycles, wagons and such need to be used on cement paths. There should be a special area in the grounds where children can dig a garden and child-sized tools should be provided for this activity. A sand pit large enough for the children to get in is desirable. This should have a cover to protect it from animals (see Figure Nineteen, p. 170).

Often it is possible to obtain a disused vehicle, remove the doors and wheels and establish it in some safe, permanent position. This will provide opportunities for good dramatic play.

Outdoor Play Equipment for an "Adventure Playground"

As with other aspects of the curriculum much will depend on the imagination and enthusiasm of the teacher. Many outdoor areas with limited possibilities have been developed into stimulating environments by creative children guided by creative teachers.

The following are suggested layouts for a preschool and a kindergarten classroom. A list of basic indoor and out-of-doors equipment is included. It should be remembered that this equipment is basic and will need to be supplemented by the teacher.

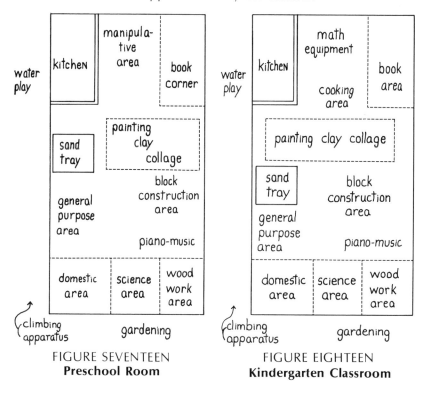

FIGURE SEVENTEEN
Preschool Room

FIGURE EIGHTEEN
Kindergarten Classroom

EQUIPMENT LISTS

Indoors:

1. Tables which are durable, stackable and have washable synthetic tops for easy cleaning.
2. Chairs which match the work tables, comfortable easy chairs for the book corner.
3. Large rug for the floor area.
4. Display shelves in the science area.

5. Benches with storage space underneath.
6. Pin-board areas on the walls.
7. Tray large enough to hold sand.
8. Piano.
9. Record player.
10. Tape Recorders.
11. Open locker for each child.
12. Area for water play.

Out-of-doors:

1. Wheel toys such as tricycles and wagons.
2. Climbing apparatus.
3. Jumping boards.
4. Strong boxes for climbing on and in.
5. Large tires.
6. Sand pit with a detachable cover.
7. Large balls.
8. Bean bags.
9. Ropes and rope ladders.
10. Area for gardening.

RECORD KEEPING OF PUPIL PROGRESS

Some kindergartens for five-year-old children are a part of the primary division of elementary schools. When this is the case more often than not the style and practice of recording pupil progress are required to be in keeping with a total school scheme. Teachers in these schools may or may not have a say in exactly what is to be recorded as evidence of pupil progress. Similarly they may or may not have an option on how pupil progress is to be recorded or when. We will here discuss record keeping of pupil progress in the light of the practices we have suggested throughout this book. If the teacher is able to begin for herself, from scratch, a scheme of systematic record keeping the suggestions we make here should be of help. If the teacher is required to operate in an existing scheme we hope these ideas and suggestions will help her record keeping to be more meaningful.

First, let us say that keeping a meaningful record of pupil progress is vital for all teachers. It is not good enough to say, as some teachers of young children do, "I keep my records in my head." Certainly there is a portion of our knowledge of each individual child which never gets put on paper. The important facets of each child's progress, however, should be documented in a meaningful way.

We have used the word "meaningful" twice in the preceding paragraph, for indeed it is the key to all sound record keeping. Meaningful to whom? To begin with it must be meaningful to the teacher who does the assessing of the pupil's progress. It must tell her precisely the story of that progress so that she can communicate it to others. Second, it has to be meaningful to other people who read the record. We are aware how meaningless have become many of the "Cumulative Record Folders" started in kindergarten and added to each year as the child progresses through elementary school. But we should ask ourselves need they become so meaningless? Similarly we are aware of how inadequate a series of numbers can become when they alone represent a record of progress (or lack of progress)— 76%, for example, means what? A credit grade? Better than average? A bare pass mark (if the pass mark is set at 75%)? A similar state of uncertainty exists with letter grading: A, B, C's and so forth. This kind of grading is fairly common in our public schools and much controversy surrounds the debate on its effectiveness as a means of assessing pupil progress, a debate which we do not want to labor here. Suffice to say that whatever is recorded has to be worthy of being recorded and the manner in which it is recorded should be as simple, straightforward and as uncluttered as possible.

Previously we suggested that the information noted by the teacher of pupil progress should be able to be communicated to others: first and foremost to parents, to other teachers who have a responsibility for the child, to the child himself, to other personnel who might be consulted (for example, about known or suspected disabilities). In this way the record becomes a diagnostic tool as well as a record of pupil attainment. Such diagnosis and attainment should cover all aspects of education: social, emotional, physical and intellectual.

Another reason for keeping records is that they assist the teacher in maintaining a sense of direction with regard to her curriculum. This is particularly necessary when the teacher operates her classroom in the manner we have suggested throughout this book. It is so easy to lose track of one's predetermined goals when operating a classroom in an open-ended way, and to lose one's goals can be fatal to sound teaching/learning. However, when goals are clearly defined, then record keeping is greatly facilitated. In this respect, the teacher can afford to broaden her teaching methods in order to enrich the learning activities she presents to her children, for she is ever mindful of the goals toward which she is working. This is the "direction" hinted at above: what to look for when assessing pupil progress, what to emphasize, what to make each child aware of in every activity pursued.

Recording of pupil progress gives written evidence of each pupil's growth and development. It is concerned with social, emotional, physical as well as intellectual and scholastic growth. It is also concerned with how the child learns and with individual differences in style, pace, time, interests. It is a record of *his* growth as an individual.

How can a teacher record, pictorially, graphically, meaningfully, the progress of young children in her care? First of all she has to nominate what learnings (concepts, facts, knowledge, skills) she wants her children to grasp. These designated learnings must be well understood by her if she is to recognize them when they become apparent. (It must be pointed out again here, that paper and pencil "tests" are not suited to young children; therefore intelligent observations of the behavior of young children is the most important way of assessing their abilities. The reader is asked to refer to Chapter Five and the anecdotal records.)

Second, the teacher must plan the activities of her class in such a way that each child will, at some time or other, be able to "show" his achievements and, as a consequence, reveal any lack of achievement.

Third, the teacher must make note or her observations. There are several methods teachers might use for noting pupil progress. These are:

1. Anecdotal records
2. Systematic observation at regular intervals using "checklists" or other diagnostic devices
3. Graphic records gathered over a period of time, e.g., intellectual development through art

Let us consider these methods in more detail.

Anecdotal Records

Anecdotal records need not be long and elaborate, for as their name implies they are short accounts of single incidents. They should be kept in folders of some kind, one folder for each child in the class.

The folders are necessary for tidiness of record keeping and to enable the contents to be readily perused so that a complete picture of each child's progress can be obtained. In and of themselves anecdotal records are not a sufficient or a complete record of pupil progress. They are, however, an excellent means of recording those spontaneous behaviors which happen day by day in a classroom of young children and which would otherwise go unrecorded. They are excellent, too, for noting the social and emotional development of children. Such records are of the kind shown in Part Two of this book, pages 111-12 in the chapter on Mathematics.

Anecdotal records should be supplemented by a more systematic observation of a child's behavior. We said earlier in this discussion that formal testing (by the traditional paper and pencil type test) is not suited to assessing the progress of young children. However, the purposes, and such features, of formalized testing procedures as can be adapted to more systematic observations and recordings will now be considered.

Systematic Observations of the
Behavior of Young Children

Probably the most useful guide for systematic observation of the behavior of young children is the checklist, such as the Readiness Check List shown on page 23 and repeated below. Checklists draw the teacher's attention to those behaviors which are pertinent to a general stage of teaching/learning or for a specific aspect of teaching/learning. For example:

1. Is the child able to converse fluently?
2. Can he communicate simple personal needs?
3. Can he listen to and carry out simple directions?
4. Can he perform skills that involve muscular coordination?
5. Can he work and play with other children without intense frustration?
6. Does he show an interest in the environment around him?
7. Is he willing to become involved in group activities, e.g., art, music, story time?
8. Can he observe with reasonable accuracy?
9. Can he concentrate on a task for a short time without undue fatigue?

10. Does he exhibit independence in selecting for himself a task he wants to work at?

A second method of systematic recording is to nominate those skills or knowledge that the teacher expects her children to acquire, tabulate them on a form and note on the form when advancements have been made by the child. For example the Language Development Chart on page 165 could be practical for four- and five-year-old children.

A third method of systematic observing of behavior is by the use of suitable standardized tests [1] administed orally. Two useful tests are the "Preschool Inventory" (Educational Testing Service, Princeton) and the "Basic Concept Inventory" (Follett Publishing Company, Chicago).

Use of Graphic Records

Such a record of a child's progress is gathered over a period of time and when consulted shows progress from the time of entry to the classroom to the present. Samples of each child's art, language (notated by the teacher if necessary), and, where appropriate, some of the child's math work, especially of the five-year-old, are particularly useful for this purpose. These records should be of the work of the individual child and be kept in folders, one for each child.

WORKING WITH PARENTS

We cannot afford not to work with parents. And we say this for several reasons. First, in the eyes of many teachers, we want to allay possible criticism of what is happening in the classroom. This factor is important especially for teachers whose practices follow those outlined in this book: practices which, while expecting good quality work from children at all times, are not designed always to obtain completed "packages" of work in alloted portions of time. A teacher might feel more comfortable about parental reactions if a child takes home each day some evidence of work (usually paper evidence) than she might if a child did not have any tangible form of evidence

---

[1] The reader is directed to *Handbook on Formative and Summative Evaluation of Student Learning* by Benjamin S. Bloom, J. Thomas Hastings, and George F. Madaus (New York: McGraw-Hill Book Co., 1971), especially to Chapter 13, "Evaluation of Learning in Preschool Education" by Constance K. Kamii. This chapter gives a very detailed account of suitable assessment precedures for preschool and kindergarten age children.

CHART ONE

Language Development Chart

Child's Name_____

ABILITY	WHEN ACHIEVED	COMMENTS
Able to understand simple directions.		
Able to listen to other children and sustain a conversation.		
Able to listen to a story appreciatively.		
Able to participate in a small group discussion.		
Able to express himself in dramatic play.		
Able to seek answers to questions.		
Acquires a larger and more varied vocabulary.		
Able to retell a well known and simple story.		
Able to take part in elementary group planning.		
Able to talk fluently about his experiences.		
Able to sustain dialogue including questioning with other children		

of the day's activities or reported to his parents that he had "played" all day. Of course the teacher knows what the child did during that day and what he meant when he reported "playing." But is the parent so aware?

Second, we need to work with parents because individually and collectively they are very talented people. We should utilize this talent to help us with our school work. Even though some of our schools have encouraged parental participation, it is more common practice to keep parents out of the classroom. A good many teachers have never thought of the excellent resources they have at their disposal. Parents have many good ideas about schools and what they are for and can do. Certainly they might need to be guided by the teacher who, as the professional educator and one alert to the many ramifications of child growth and development, has the responsibility for the soundness of the curriculum of the class. This responsibility she cannot ever abdicate.

Third, as a teacher who meets each child for only a few hours every school day, there is a large gap in her understanding of that child. What does the child do at home? How does he behave? What are his interests? Who does he play with? Many questions such as these can best be answered by parents and they need to be communicated to the teacher if she is to gain a reasonable and complete picture of a "whole" child. Teachers need each parent's knowledge of their children.

As teachers and school personnel we have been saying for a long time that we need to work with parents, in and through the homes. Pestalozzi, Froebel, Dewey, to name but a few educators, have advised us over the past years not to ignore the homes of the children. Today many of the "experimental" [2] early childhood programs have, once again, brought to the forefront of educational thinking the necessity for sound home-school relationships. It is easy for us to say that children need adults, and they need the support of their parents. This support is needed in their school life too, for school is important to children, second in importance only to their home. The big question for many teachers is how to get this support, and for some teachers this is difficult.

The first thing for teachers to realize is that parents, too, are individuals. Some parents will readily contribute to the life of the school (indeed some will want to over-contribute). Other parents

[2] Two examples are "The Florida Parent-Education Model" developed by Ira Gordon at the University of Florida and "The Early Childhood Center" of the Bank Street College of Education in New York City.

will be reluctant to contribute and will need some coaxing and in many cases will need to be made to feel adequate for whatever the classroom activity might be. Some parents teachers seldom see, if ever. This is unfortunate for it creates a considerable problem for teachers of the young who see the urgency of good home-school relationships. In some instances both parents are working and are seldom home or have the time for developing relationships with their child's school. In other cases the parents (or parent) are plainly just not interested. Not so long ago when teachers lived in the neighborhood where they taught, they could meet the reticent parent at the laundromat, or at the supermarket or similar communal meeting place. But it is not so easy to do this now, especially in the larger cities where teachers live in one suburb and the school is in another—often miles away. We think, though, it is true to say that most parents have a genuine interest in their children and their children's school, and teachers must capitalize on this interest.

Parents have to be made to feel welcome in the classroom. Teachers of preschool and kindergarten children have an opportunity to get parents to bring their children right to the classroom each morning and not just to the school gate. Once at the door it is not far to "Come inside and see what Johnnie made yesterday." Parents should be encouraged at the end of the day to collect their children at the classroom, not at the gate or parking lot. Such short meetings are invaluable for both parent and teacher.

In cases where parents do not bring their children to school the teacher must make every endeavor to *communicate* with those parents in some way. Generally the initiative in this matter rests with the teacher. The mode of the communication will depend upon the circumstances in each case. It might be done by telephone or a home visit after school or at weekends, or even by an arranged "casual" meeting. The memorandum, dittoed-off and pinned to each child's clothing, is not a sufficiently personal means of communication, though it does help in keeping some parents alerted to the happenings of the class.

Once contact has been made with parents and a line of communication has been begun, the teacher has to be clear in her mind how she wants to use this communication and for what purposes. Again we should look at common practices of working with parents. Parent Teacher Associations are one way of getting parents involved in the life of their schools, but in many respects this involvement is fairly peripheral and usually concerned with fund raising. This should not even be the first consideration of the teacher. Rather, it is the parent as the mother or father of a child in her class, as a fellow educator of that child, that the teacher should be considering.

"What can we do in the classroom with all these parents?" teachers ask. This is a very real problem for many teachers. Some add: "We just haven't time to tell them what to do as well as attend to what we have to do." This problem is very real, and there is no easy answer to questions such as these. If we agree that we want parents to become an important part of the classroom then we have to be prepared to have them there. Being prepared means having something for them to do. And this doesn't mean saving up those tedious tasks such as cutting paper or cloth, mixing paints, cleaning out this or that cupboard (the children are capable of doing many of these tasks and enjoy doing so). Certainly parents will gladly assist with the "chores" provided they are balanced with activities of a more meaningful kind. It is in this regard that teachers must utilize the *talents* of parents. What are parents interested in and very good at doing?·Sewing? Clay modelling? Knitting? Breeding fish? Gardening? Cooking? Astronomy? Antique collecting? There is such a diversity of interests and talents among each parent body that if only teachers would care to ask parents what *they* would like to do to contribute to the class's learning environment there should result a most enriched learning environment.

We all know that interests are infectious especially if "propagated" by an expert in that field. Why shouldn't a parent who is keen, say on collecting coins, be able to contribute to a group of interested children's understanding of time, number, history, geography, language and so on? It is so with the interested knitter, cook, collector, gardener—they can excite children and enrich their experiences in many ways and in doing so *complement* the talents and expertise of the teacher.

The experience-oriented approach to curriculum design we have developed in this book enables parents and other adults, youth and children to become involved as valuable resources in the work of the classroom. Of course, such resource personnel need to be planned for and programmed into the selected activities offered the children. With the children of such classes working in groups for most of their activities the parents, who in most cases are untrained as teachers, have less fear of not being able to manage than they would have if asked to work with the whole class. If the teacher is, however, maintaining a tight inflexible control over the activities of the class, then the utilization of parents and other helpers in the classroom could become an added chore to an already overloaded (even if self-inflicted) list of responsibilities.

One further aspect of working with parents which we want the reader to consider is the importance of home visits especially to those parents who seldom come into the school and classroom. Some current programs in early childhood have regular home visitations as an integral part of their total program. Here the teacher and aide, or as exemplified in the Florida Parent Educator Model mentioned earlier a special "parent educator," pay regular visits, usually one each week, to the homes of their children. On these home visits they take with them a "task" or "learning activity" which the parent can help the child do during the following week. Such a task or learning activity is intended to be within the ability of the parent to develop and is connected to the interests of the child and his work at school. Not all parents need such "tasks" or "learning activities" but for the less capable parent it is a reasonably effective means of getting the parent actively involved with the education of her child.

We will summarize this discussion on working with parents by reiterating that, first it is vital that teachers of the young child work *with* parents wherever and whenever possible. Indeed, in this regard the initiative has to be ours. We must actively seek the support and contribution of parents to the education we are providing their children. Wherever possible we should bring the parents into the school so that a better understanding of the goals of education will develop. Where the bringing of parents into the school is not possible then aspects of the school have to be taken into the homes of the children. This could mean home visitations at any time, even at weekends.

Second, once communication with the home has been established then parents need to be *involved* in an active way in the education of their children. It is up to the teacher to utilize the talents of each parent in widening the opportunities for experiencing what she presents to her children.

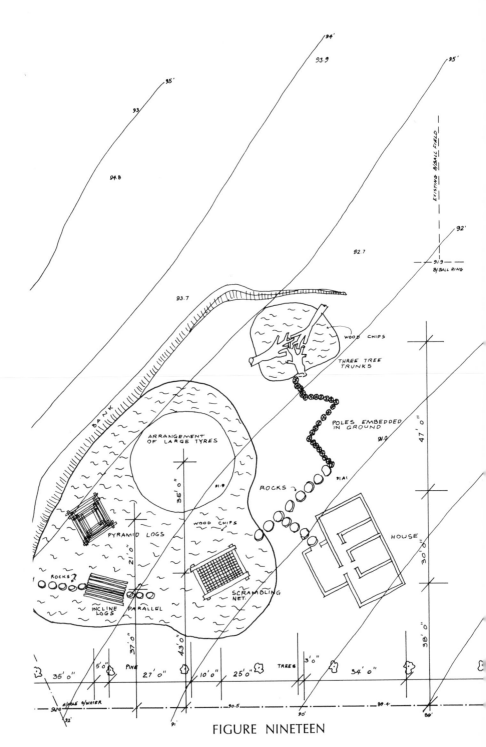

FIGURE NINETEEN

170

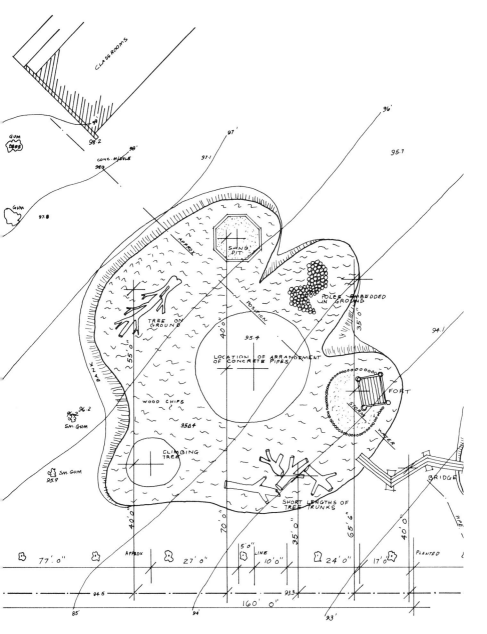

CLASSROOMS

GUM
98.5

98.2

CONC. MIDDLE
98.0

97'

97.1

97'

96'

95.7

GUM
97.8

APPROX

SWING
PIT

POSITION

POLES EMBEDDED
IN GROUND

35' 0"

94.1

TREE ON
GROUND

40' 0"

95.4

LOCATION OF ARRANGEMENT
OF CONCRETE PIPES

BANK

55' 0"

96.2
96.2
SM. GUM

WOOD CHIPS

95.4

STORM

WATER

FORT

BRIDGE

SM. GUM
95.9

CLIMBING
TREE

40' 0"

70' 0"

35' 0"

65' 6"

40' 0"

SHORT LENGTHS OF
TREE TRUNKS

PIPE

77' 0"

APPROX

27' 0"

5' 0"

LINE

10' 0"

24' 0"

17' 0"

PLANTED

94.5

85'

94'

93.3

93'

93'

160' 0"

171

APPENDIX A

Bibliography of Children's Books

Author	Book Name	Publisher
Anglund, Joan	*A Friend Is Someone Who Likes You*	Harcourt, Brace, Jovanovich
Barry, Katharine	*A Bug to Hug*	Harcourt, Brace, Jovanovich
Bemelmans, Ludwig	*Madeline and the Gypsies* *Madeline's Rescue*	Viking Press
Budney, Blosom	*A Kiss Is Round*	Harper & Row
Burton, Virginia Lee	*The Little House* *Mike Mulligan and His Steam Shovel*	Houghton Mifflin Co.
Carle, Eric	*The Very Hungry Caterpillar*	Hamish Hamilton
Carrol, Ruth	*Where's The Bunny?* *Where's the Kitty?*	Oxford University Press
Cole, William	*Frances Face-Maker*	World Publishing Co.
Cook, Bernadine	*The Curious Kitten* *The Fish That Got Away* *Looking for Susie*	Young Scott Books
Dillon, Ina K.	*Policeman*	Melmont Publishing Co.
Dubasing, Roger	*The House of Four Seasons*	Lothrop, Lee, & Shephard
Dugan, William	*The Ball Book* *The Bus Book* *The Truck Book*	Golden Press

Author	Book Name	Publisher
Earle, Vana	The Busy Man and the Night Time Noises	Lothrop, Lee, & Shepherd
Eggleston, Joyce Smith	Things That Grow	Melmont Publishing Co.
Ets, Marie Hall	Play with Me	Viking Press
Flack, Marjorie	Angus (Series) New Pet Wag-Tail Bess	Doubleday & Co.
Francoise	Jeanne-Marie Counts Her Sheep	Charles Scribner's Sons
Freeman, Don	Mop-Top	Children's Press
Gag, Wanda	Millions of Cats	Coward, McCann, & Geoghegan
Gay, Zhenya	What's Your Name?	Viking Press
Gibson, Morrell	Hello Peter	Doubleday & Co.
Green, Mary McBurney	Everybody Has a House	William R. Scott, Inc.
Heffelfinger, Jane and Hoffman, E.	About Firemen About Our Friendly Helper	Melmont Publishing Co.
Holland, Marion	A Big Ball of String	Random House
Howell, Rea	Everything Changes	Atheneum Publishers
Howell, Virginia	Who Likes the Dark	Howell, Soskin Publishing Co.
Jackson, Kathryn	Wheels	Golden Press
Keats, Ezra Jack	Peter's Chair The Snowy Day Whistle for Willie	Harper & Row Viking Press Viking Press
Kraus, Ruth	The Bundle Book The Carrot Seed The Growing Story A Hole Is to Dig A Very Special House	Harper & Row
Leaf, Munro	Boo Ferdinand	Random House
Lenski, Lois	"Little" Series "Small" Series	Henry Z. Walck, Inc.

Author	Book Name	Publisher
Martin, Dick	The Apple Book The Fish Book The Sand Pail Book	Golden Press
Mayer, Mercer	A Boy, A Dog, and a Frog	Dial Press
McCloskey, Robert	Blueberries for Sal Lentil Make Way for Ducklings	Follett Publishing Co.
Munari, Bruno	Animals for Sale	World Publishing Co.
Nodset, Joan	Go Away, Dog	Harper & Row
Ormsby, Virginia	It's Saturday	J. B. Lippincott & Co.
Parkes, Gale	Here Comes Daddy	William R. Scott, Inc.
Parsons, Virginia	Homes Night	Garden City Books
Paull, Grace	Someday	Abelard Schuman
Pfloog, Jan	The Bear Book The Cat Book The Dog Book The Fox Book	Golden Press
Potter, Beatrix	The Tale of Peter Rabbit	Frederick Warne & Co.
Rand, Ann	The Little River	Harcourt, Brace, Jovanovich
Rice, Inez	A Long, Long Time	Lothrop, Lee, & Shepherd
Rye, H. A.	Curious George Flies a Kite	Houghton Mifflin
Schlein, Miriam	How Do You Travel? Shapes	Abington Press
Sendak, Maurice	One Way Johnny	Harper & Row
Slobodkina, Esphyr	Caps for Sale The Clock	William R. Scott, Inc. E. M. Hale & Co.
Smith, Eunice Y.	The Little Red Drum	Albert Whitman & Co.
Thompson, Frances B.	About Doctor John	Melmont Publishing Co.

Author	Book Name	Publisher
Tudor, Tasha	Mother Goose	Oxford University Press
	1 Is One	Henry Z. Walck, Inc.
Udry, Janice May	Let's Be Enemies	Harper & Row
	A Tree Is Nice	
Ungerer, Tom	Snail, Where Are You?	Harper & Row
Wagner, Peggy	Hurrah for Hats	Children's Press
Wildsmith, Brian	Brian Wildsmith's Birds	Franklin Watts, Inc.
	The Hare and the Tortoise	
	Mother Goose Puzzles	
Wright, Ethel	Saturday Flight	William R. Scott, Inc.
	Saturday Ride	
	Saturday Walk	
Yashimo, Taro	Umbrella	Viking Press
	The Village Tree	
Zion, Gene	All Falling Down	Harper & Row
	Dear Garbage Man	
	Harry and the Lady Next Door	
	Harry the Dirty Dog	
	No Roses for Harry	
	The Plant Sitter	
	Really Spring	
Zolotow, Charlotte	One Step, Two . . .	Lothrop, Lee, & Shepherd
	The Park Book	Harper & Row
	The Sky Was Blue	Harper & Row
	Sleepy Book	Lothrop, Lee, & Shepherd
	Someday	Lothrop, Lee, & Shepherd
	The Storm Book	Harper & Row

APPENDIX B

Recipes Suitable for Use in Classrooms

HOMEMADE BREAD

Ingredients: 1¼ cups lukewarm water
1 packet yeast
1 cup milk—scalded
2 tablespoons sugar
2 teaspoons salt
2 tablespoons shortening
7 to 7½ cups sifted flour

Method: 1. Dissolve yeast and 1 teaspoon sugar in ¼ cup luke-warm water taken from above amount. Let stand 10 minutes.

2. Scald milk. Add sugar, salt, water and shortening. Cool to lukewarm.

3. Add yeast mixture and flour gradually, beating thoroughly after each addition.

4. Turn dough out on a lightly floured board and knead until smooth—about 10 minutes.

5. Shape into a ball and place in a greased bowl. Brush lightly with melted shortening. Cover. Let rise until double in bulk, about 1½ hours.

6. Divide into two portions. Shape into loaves and place in two greased breadpans. Brush top lightly with shortening. Cover. Let rise until double in size.

Bake at 375° F for approximately 50 minutes.

HOMEMADE CONDENSED MILK

Ingredients: 1½ pints fresh milk
1½ lbs. sugar
2½ tablespoons corn starch

Method: Boil the milk and while boiling add the sugar. Stir until sugar has dissolved. Stir in the corn starch made into a paste with a little milk. Boil for a few minutes.

BUTTERMILK CHEESE

Ingredients: Pint of buttermilk
Salt

Method: Allow buttermilk to stand until thick. Stir in salt to taste and place mixture in a muslin bag. Hang and allow to drip.
Will be ready in 6 days.

FRUIT SALAD JAM

Ingredients: 1 lb. apricots
1 lb. peaches
2 bananas
1 lemon
½ lb. apples
½ lb. plums
3½ lb. sugar

Method: 1. Slice apricots, peaches and plums, add diced apple, sliced bananas, juice of the lemon and 1 teaspoon of grated lemon rind.

2. Cook the fruit for a few minutes until tender, stirring often.

3. Add the sugar and stir until dissolved.

4. Boil quickly till mixture sets when tested (approximately 30 minutes).
   Cooking Test: If a few drops of syrup thickens when placed on a saucer then the jam is cooked.

PLAIN CAKE

Ingredients: ¼ lb. shortening
1 cup sugar
½ cup milk
1½ cups flour
1½ teaspoons baking powder
2 eggs
Few drops of vanilla essence

Method: Cream butter and sugar, beat in one egg and beat, then add the other egg. Add milk and flour alternately. Add vanilla. Bake in a greased pan ¾ hour at 350°.

MERINGUES

Ingredients: Greased paper
4 ozs. powdered sugar
2 egg whites

Method: Whisk whites of eggs until very stiff. Beat in half the sugar, fold in remainder carefully and gently. Place spoonfuls of the mixture on to the tray lined with greased paper. Place tray in a cool oven for 2-3 hours, until shapes are firm and crisp.

CUPCAKES

Ingredients: 4 ozs. shortening
½ cup sugar
2 eggs
1 teaspoon vanilla
½ cup of milk
2 cups of self rising flour

Method: Cream shortening and sugar. Add eggs. Add vanilla. Add milk and flour. Cook in cupcake pans approximately 20 minutes at 375°.

Note: This mixture can be cooked in a frypan using an asbestos mat and individual foil cupcake cups. Cook 375° approximately 45 minutes.

DOUGHNUTS

Ingredients: 2 cups flour
¼ cup sugar
3 teaspoons baking powder
½ teaspoon salt
¼ cup cooking oil

¾ cup of milk
egg

Method: Sift together the dry ingredients. Mix together the oil, milk and egg, and add to the dry ingredients. Drop by teaspoonful into hot fat, 375° F. Cook for approximately 3 minutes. Drain and shake into a bag of sugar.

PEANUT COOKIES

Ingredients: 4 oz. shortening
1 egg
pinch of salt
2 teaspoons drinking chocolate
½ lb. raw peanuts
1 cup sugar
1 cup flour
1 teaspoon baking powder

Method: Cream butter and sugar, add beaten egg, then the dry ingredients. Lastly add nuts and vanilla. Drop by teaspoonful on to a greased oven tray. Bake at 350° for approximately 20 minutes.

NO-BAKE HEDGE-HOG SLICES

Ingredients: 4 ozs. butter
4 ozs. confectioner's sugar
1 tablespoon of cocoa
Bring to boil and add:
1 beaten egg
1 cup of raisins
½ lb. broken cookies

Method: Stir all ingredients well. Press into a tin and leave in the refrigerator one hour. Ice with chocolate icing and sprinkle with coconut.

BUMBLE BEES

Ingredients: 1 cup coconut
1¼ cup raisins

1 cup dates
1 cup nuts
½ can condensed milk
½ cup of flour
extra coconut
cherries

Method: Chop up the dates, nuts and raisins. Add raisins and coconut, then condensed milk, mixing all well together. Mold
a teaspoonful at a time, roll into balls, roll in coconut and
top with a piece of cherry. Place on a greased tray. Bake
at 350° for 15-20 minutes.

SIMPLE COOKIE MIXTURE

Ingredients: 4 cups flour
½ cup confectioner's sugar
8 ozs. shortening
2 egg yolks
4 tablespoons water

Method: Sift flour and icing sugar into a bowl. Rub in butter
until mixture resembles fine bread crumbs. Make a well
in the center of dry ingredients, add egg yolks and
water. Mix to firm dough. Roll out thinly on floured
surface. Cut into shapes designed by children. Bake
in moderate oven 12 to 15 minutes.

SHORTBREAD

Ingredients: ½ lb. shortening
4 ozs. powdered sugar
1 lb. flour

Method: Cream shortening and sugar. Add flour. Press into a
tray and prick with a fork. Bake in a slow oven approximately one hour. Slice into fingers.

OLD FASHIONED SUGAR COOKIES

Ingredients: ¾ cup margarine
1 cup sugar

1 egg
⅓ cup of milk
3 cups sifted flour
1 teaspoon soda
½ teaspoon salt
2 teaspoons vanilla

Method: Cream margarine and sugar. Add the egg and milk. Blend in the sifted dry ingredients, vanilla and mix well again. Either roll this dough out and use cookie cutters or form into small balls and flatten on the baking tray. Bake for approximately 10 minutes at 375°.

CANDY

Creamy Coconut Ice

Ingredients: 1 lb. sifted powdered sugar
½ lb. coconut
½ teaspoon vanilla
2 slightly beaten egg whites
4 ozs. melted shortening
Red food coloring

Method: Mix all ingredients thoroughly and divide mixture in half. Color one half pink. Press one color mixture into a greased paper lined cake tin. Place other mixture on top. Refrigerate until firm and then cut into squares.

Fudge

Ingredients: 1 can condensed milk
5 tablespoons water
1 teaspoon of vanilla
Pinch of cream of tartar
2 lbs. sugar
3 tablespoons powdered chocolate
¼ lb. shortening

Method: Boil all ingredients except vanilla and cream of tartar for 10 minutes, stirring all the time. Remove from heat add cream of tartar and vanilla. Beat until thick. Refrigerate until set and cut into shapes.

Caramels

Ingredients: 1 can condensed milk
4 ozs. margarine
½ lb. sugar
½ teaspoon vanilla

Method: Boil all ingredients except vanilla for 15 minutes. Add vanilla. Pour into greased tray and refrigerate. Cut when cool.

Toffee

Ingredients: 1 lb. white sugar
¼ pint water
1 tablespoon vanilla
1 oz. butter

Method: Combine ingredients and boil without stirring to the brittle stage. Pour into a buttered tin. Break into pieces when cool.

Note: To test for right consistency drop a small amount of the boiled mixture into cold water. If it hardens then it's done.

Toffee Apples (Candy Apples)

Ingredients: 4 cups water
1 cup sugar
2 tablespoons vinegar
2 tablespoons glucose
red coloring
Firm apples (fresh)

Method: Boil ingredients without stirring, to the brittle stage. Dip apple skewered on to a stick into the toffee and allow to set.

Quick Toffee Mixture

Ingredients: 1 lb. sugar
3 tablespoons vinegar or lemon juice

Method: Place ingredients in pan and bring to the boil. Allow to boil until mixture becomes honey colored—about 5 minutes. Pour into a greased pan and allow to set.

Honey Toffee

Ingredients: 1 lb. sugar
1 lb. honey
3 oz. margarine

Method: Combine all ingredients and stir until mixture boils. Do not stir once mixture boils. Allow to boil until brittle.

JELLO JUBES

Ingredients: 1 oz. gelatin
1 lb. sugar
½ pint water
Pinch citric acid
Coloring
Powdered sugar

Method: Soak gelatin in a little of the water, and soak sugar in the remainder of the water. Place in a large saucepan and stir until boiling. Boil gently for 20 minutes. Remove from heat and color. Pour into greased dishes and cut into squares when cold and set. Roll in powdered sugar.

MARSHMALLOWS

Ingredients: 2 ozs. gelatin
2 lbs. sugar
2½ cups water
Coloring and flavoring
Coconut or powdered sugar

Method: Soak gelatin in one cup of water. Place the remainder of water with the sugar in a pan and bring to the boil. Add the soaked gelatin and boil for 20 minutes. Allow to cool slightly, add flavoring (few drops) and beat the mixture until very thick. Pour into greased tins and allow to set. When set cut into squares. Can be rolled in coconut or powdered sugar.

Peanut Crunch

Ingredients: 4 ozs. shortening
1 cup sugar
2 tablespoons honey
½ cup of coconut
½ cup raw peanuts
4 cups rice bubbles

Method: Heat butter, sugar, honey for 5 minutes. Pour over dry ingredients. Mix well, then put into a greased flat pan and mark into squares. Cool in a refrigerator.

Sugar-Coated Peanuts

Ingredients: ½ lb. raw peanuts
1 cup water
1 cup sugar
½ teaspoon red coloring

Method: Combine all ingredients into a frypan (electric). DO NOT STIR AT ALL. Shake pan a little to distribute the food coloring. Boil steadily for 10 minutes without stirring. Remove from heat. Stir with a fork until peanuts become sugar coated. Turn out and cool on tray.

Index

INDEX

Activity, 16, 25, 31, 52
Art, 86-102:
  collage, 100
  drawing, 94
  environment, 87, 88, 89
  experiences, 94-101
  finger painting, 96-99
  manipulative stage, 86-87
  modeling, 99-100
  painting, 94-96
  puppetry, 101
  symbolic stage, 87
Associating experiences, 17

Block play, 65-66

Centers of interest, 106, 111-12, 168-69
Central theme, 41, 47, 106, 149-54, 168-69
Children's story books, 171-76
Classroom organization, 154
Concept development, 14, 25, 108-10
Cooking recipes, 177-87
Curriculum, 143

Daily planning, 148
Displays, 125
Domestic area, 82-83
Drama, 70, 82-85

Environment, 105-39:
  physical, 49, 105, 154-60
  school, 32, 47, 52, 87, 105-15, 133, 154-60, 163
  social, 132-39
Environmental influences, 3, 16, 31, 52:
  familial, 4, 33, 164-69
  cultural, 4, 10, 14
Experiential background, 32, 47, 108, 118

Field trips, 42, 126-28
Furniture, materials for, 155-56

Individual differences, 3-5, 37:
  in abilities, 4, 36, 37
  in interests, 4, 7, 17, 31, 43
  in personality, 3
  in physical appearance, 3
Integrated day, 144-48

Language, 35-38, 38-42:
  auditory and visual discrimination, 48, 49
  development of, 35
  games to aid, 38-40
  language experience approach, 52-53
  literature and, 171-76
  motor coordination and, 48

Language *(Continued)*
  oral communication and, 48
  reading and, 45-49
  sensory development and,
    50-51
  vocabulary and, 36, 37
  written, 45
Learning, 3, 5, 15-19:
  activity in, 16-23
  curiosity and, 16-23, 32,
    118-21
  experience and, 17-19, 24
  motives for, 5-7, 26
  play and, 8
  repetition and, 19
  subjects and, 31
Literature, 42-49, 51:
  and pictures, 37

Mathematics, 108-15:
  concepts of, 108-11
  materials and, 113-14
Motivation, 5-8, 17, 21, 23, 52
Movement, 70-74, 79-81
Music, 70-74, 74-79:
  listening to, 78
  making music, 76-78
  singing, 74

Nature, 41, 125:
  area, 41, 126

Outdoor materials, 156-60

Paraprofessionals, 47, 166
Parents, 164-69
Play, 8-15, 63-67, 82, 135:
  as therapy, 8-10
  directed, 12, 13, 14-15
  in cognitive development, 12,
    38

  in emotional development,
    11-12
  in the socialization of the
    child, 10-12, 47, 135
  spontaneous, 12-15

Readiness, 19-23:
  checklist for, 20, 23
  definition of, 19
  emergence of, 19
  experiential background of,
    22, 32
  for reading, 20-21, 42-43, 51
  maturity and, 22
  motivation and, 23
Reading, 45-63:
  beginning, 45
  in kindergarten, 51-63
  in nursery schools, 45
  readiness, 45, 46
Record keeping, 160-64

Sandbox play, 64-65
Science, 116-31:
  explorations and, 118-21
  materials for, 128-30
  recording, 128
Sensory experiences, 41, 117
Social development, 47, 105,
    132-39
Story-telling, 43

Teaching practices, 23-27, 44,
    47, 52, 71-74, 75-76, 105,
    136-37, 144, 165:
  atmosphere, 25-26, 52
  encouragement, 27
  materials, 25
  stimulation, 26, 52
Touch-table, 41
Toys, 67

Water play, 63-64
Woodworking, 66-67
Written communication, 45, 63:
 reading, 45-63
 writing, 63-68